T0285303

NIKKI KINZER, PCC AND PETE D. WRIGHT

Unapologetically
ADHD

A STEP-BY-STEP FRAMEWORK FOR
EVERYDAY PLANNING ON YOUR TERMS

WILEY

Published by John Wiley & Sons, Inc., Hoboken, New Jersey.
Published simultaneously in Canada.

For general information on our other products and services or for technical support, please contact our Customer Care Department within the United States at (800) 762-2974, outside the United States at (317) 572-3993 or fax (317) 572-4002.

Wiley also publishes its books in a variety of electronic formats. Some content that appears in print may not be available in electronic formats. For more information about Wiley products, visit our web site at www.wiley.com.

Library of Congress Cataloging-in-Publication Data:

Names: Kinzer, Nikki, author. | Wright, Pete D., author.
Title: Unapologetically ADHD : a step-by-step framework for everyday
   planning on your own terms / Nikki Kinzer and Pete Wright.
Description: Hoboken, New Jersey : Wiley, [2024] | Includes bibliographical
   references and index.
Identifiers: LCCN 2024014799 (print) | LCCN 2024014800 (ebook) | ISBN
   9781394265428 (hardback) | ISBN 9781394265442 (adobe pdf) | ISBN
   9781394265435 (epub)
Subjects: LCSH: People with attention-deficit hyperactivity disorder—Life
   skills guides. | Attention-deficit hyperactivity disorder in
   adults—Popular works. | Attention-deficit hyperactivity
   disorder—Popular works. | Personal coaching—Popular works.
Classification: LCC RC394.A85 K56 2024 (print) | LCC RC394.A85 (ebook) |
   DDC 616.85/89—dc23/eng/20240411
LC record available at https://lccn.loc.gov/2024014799
LC ebook record available at https://lccn.loc.gov/2024014800

Cover Design: Wiley
Cover Image: © blankstock/Adobe Stock Photos
Author Photo: Courtesy of Brad Kinzer
SKY10079415_071224

To all those with ADHD who see the world differently

This book is for the creative spirits, restless minds, outside-the-box thinkers, and trailblazers who refuse to see their ADHD as making them feel less than. For too long, society has said something is wrong with how your brain is wired.

This is a call to all who refuse to hide their lightning-fast thoughts, endless curiosity, and indomitable spirit. Through these pages, we inspire you to start living unapologetically—to feel pride rather than shame in how you experience the world.

Success isn't linear; the most remarkable breakthroughs happen when convention is disrupted. We hope the strategies and stories in these pages help you celebrate your uniqueness and use your diverse skills to change the world in your own remarkable way. Most of all, we hope this book reminds you that you were destined for greatness just as you are.

Contents

Foreword

When Nikki Kinzer and Pete Wright first approached me about writing a foreword for their book on planning, prioritizing, and evaluating for those diagnosed with ADHD, I felt deeply honored. These two have been dear colleagues and friends for years, pioneering the podcast world with their incredibly popular show, *Taking Control: The ADHD Podcast*, which has helped so many navigate the realities and challenges of ADHD.

To be considered for their "Hall of Fame" as a frequent guest is a truly humbling honor that I can't help but poke fun at—one they would absolutely appreciate with their trademark senses of humor. That same warmth, deep insight, and captivating storytelling they bring to the airwaves shines through in this book.

As a professional who has specialized in treating ADHD for over three decades, I can attest to the monumental challenge that executive skill deficits pose. The inability to plan, prioritize tasks, and evaluate what deserves our focus creates relentless overwhelm and paralysis. I've witnessed innumerable bright and capable individuals hobbled by executive skill deficits where goals go unmet, and dreams get deferred—all because of ADHD's insidious disruption of our brain's command center.

That's why I'm so grateful Nikki and Pete have dedicated their considerable expertise to this notoriously difficult domain. With hard-earned wisdom forged in their own different ADHD journeys, they craft a roadmap through executive dysfunction that is both compassionate and practical.

What makes this book so powerful is how it blends invaluable psychoeducation about the neurological underpinnings of executive dysfunction with highly personalized, real-world strategies and tools. Their innovative "Workbox" concept empowers each person to customize their own systems instead of fruitlessly trying to adopt ones that don't fit their unique needs. I believe personalization is a vital element in learning to master these executive system challenges. Readers will arrive at an understanding of why their brains work the way they do, while learning to navigate the shame and stigma that so often accompany ADHD.

This book's greatest strength is preparing you for the harsh realities and uphill battles ahead, while inspiring the unshakable belief that you can, in fact, develop strategies to manage executive functioning. They provide great compassion for how foreign and uncomfortable new routines can feel, balanced with a conviction that your potential is limitless when we embrace our unique neurology. Their narrative resonates with hope, determination, and the incredible freedom that comes from developing strategies for managing planning, prioritizing, and evaluating.

This book is written by those who get it, for those who need it most. I recommend this book to any member of the ADHD tribe still struggling to rein in chaos and reclaim their personal power around planning, prioritizing, and evaluating. Even for those who may have a grasp on these issues, the book offers a uniquely fresh perspective to gain insight into this lifelong challenge. I am proud to say Nikki and Pete have created a guide to transforming the world of ADHD, one prioritized action at a time. This book will be a long-standing resource, and one that readers will turn to time and time again.

—James Ochoa, LPC

Author of *Focused Forward: Navigating the Storms of Adult ADHD*

Introduction

Hi, I'm Nikki Kinzer.

I am a certified ADHD coach, podcaster, writer, teacher, and business owner, and I have dedicated my life's work to working with adults with ADHD, and I love it. I'm a daughter, sister, aunt, wife, mother, and friend. I love puzzles and red barns. My favorite number is 10, and I love chocolate peanut butter ice cream.

In 2008, I started an organizing business and became a professional organizer. I asked Pete if he could help me with my website, and he agreed, and we've been working together since. Two years later, I changed the direction of my business to focus only on ADHD. Together, we provide a unique perspective on common ADHD struggles.

Our partnership is unique. Pete comes from the perspective of living with ADHD, and I come from the perspective of an ADHD coach. I do not have ADHD; my personal experience comes from working with hundreds of clients over the last 15-plus years, and I am a mother to a daughter with ADHD.

This book is written in a style similar to our podcast. I share what I've learned over many years about planning with ADHD. Pete is a great storyteller and often uses metaphors in his descriptions when sharing his own knowledge and experience with ADHD.

Our mission for the podcast has always been to raise awareness of ADHD and inspire those who listen. That is our same mission here. We hope you walk away with a planning system, but more than anything, we hope you stop feeling the need to apologize for your ADHD. Give yourself permission to design the life you want to live.

You are enough. You are worthy. You are unapologetically ADHD.

Hi, I'm Pete Wright

I'm a podcaster, business owner, writer, designer, photographer, and constant cohabitator with ADHD and anxiety. That makes for a complicated bouquet of competing sensory experiences that anyone staking out their homestead in the wilds of the neurodiversity spectrum might find familiar. At least, that's my hope. Yikes. It also reads just like a career someone with ADHD might cobble together.

When Nikki and I started our show, *Taking Control: The ADHD Podcast*, in 2010, it wasn't an ADHD podcast. It was an organizing podcast with attention issues. But Nikki was an organizing coach back then, and I was a humble podcaster with a fondness for office supplies. A little while into our production, we discovered two things. First, Nikki loved working with people with ADHD the *most*. Second, I got to surprise her with my very own adult ADHD diagnosis, and as if delivered from high up on the mountaintop, we realized that it was time to stop pretending we loved organizing alone and start talking directly to the people we loved the most.

In this book, we hope you're going to find the same healthy mix of worldviews that you get from us on the podcast. But don't worry; you don't need to have heard a single episode of the show to get something out of what we're doing in this book. Nikki has spent years working with ADHDers, crafting a practice of planning and organizing that is free of judgment and shame that not only works for the ADHD brain but is resilient to the challenges that ADHD throws at it. For my part, I'd like to give you a tour of how I think and feel when faced with these sorts of systems and how I celebrate when I am able to stare down the grizzliest of my ADHD challenges. Or hide from them. Like, under my bed. Because who are we kidding? That's ADHD, too.

Before we get going, here are a few quick notes. First, I don't know who you are out there reading this, so I have decided to call you Jordan. If you read that I am talking about Jordan, it's because I'm talking to you.

Second, you might be asking, "Pete, how will I know when you're writing and when Nikki is teaching me the important stuff?" Great question, Jordan (see that? I'm already doing it). You'll know something is coming from me when it shows up in a box, just like the one you're reading right now. The Pete Box. When you see it, you know you're in for a little break between concepts, and you can give yourself a chance to slow down and just relate for a few pages.

Finally, I want to say thank you, Jordan. Opening another book on planning (because there's *always* another book on planning) when you're living with even a dash of the ADHD spice is a massive accomplishment. Thank you for showing up, thank you for joining us, and thank you for believing that what we have to share is different. This work has made a difference in our lives and might just make a difference in your life, too.

What Is the Framework?

One reason many people with ADHD go through several calendars, planners, and task managers is that the tools aren't seen as one complete planning system with interconnected components. Instead, they are being used as stand-alone pieces, and there hasn't been a clear workflow established for how these systems work together.

A complete planning system is like a well-oiled machine: each component works in harmony with the others to manage your time and keep track of your tasks.

The framework we provide is based on weekly and daily planning. The mission is to build and customize your own system. The system includes planning tools like a calendar and task manager *and* the actions needed to maintain the tools.

The planning system supports your ADHD and is resilient enough not to break when things don't go as planned. (Spoiler alert: plans rarely go as planned.) But that's OK because your system is flexible. You expect plans to change because, in this process, you have learned to reframe your approach to planning.

Below is a summary of how the book is organized and what to expect in each chapter.

How to Read This Book

When you build a house, you start with laying the foundation. Once the foundation is set, it's time to frame the structure. Then you need to enclose the structure and add any additional touches. The final step is to decorate the house and make it your home. You can't make it your home until the previous steps are completed.

Building and customizing your planning system is like building a house. Working through each of the steps is what separates a complete planning system from a few random planning tools.

Each chapter builds upon the previous chapter. Read through it once from start to finish to ensure you have a handle on the concepts. After that, have at it. You're free to jump around as you please.

The intention of this book is not to be a passive read; it's a book where, at the end of each chapter, exercises will be designed to prepare you for the next chapter. Take your time and be prepared to answer several questions through various worksheets. You will be asked to go deeper in your thought process than you might do on your own. We do this inner work by being curious and reframing our approach to planning.

Pete and I have developed a soft way of talking about planning. What I mean is that it takes away the expectations, standards, and negative stigma that many with ADHD feel when they think about planning anything. We have a framework to teach; it's not perfect, and you will still have ADHD when it's built. However, you will no longer have to be anyone else than who you are.

Glossary of Terms

To keep planning interesting and not something that you want to run away from every time you see the word, we created a new glossary of terms:

- **Workbox:** This is the central hub where your work is organized and tracked. It includes your primary calendar, task manager, and other planning tools.
- **Inbox:** This is the temporary holding space for new information before entering it into your workbox.
- **Workflow:** These are the action steps involved in updating and maintaining your workbox and overall planning system. Workflows are similar to routines.
- **Weekly Focus:** Your planning workflow to maintain your workbox is conducted during the weekly focus session.
- **Daily Detour:** A daily check-in is performed to preview the day ahead and make necessary adjustments.

Following is a quick rundown of what you have to look forward to as you read on.

Part 1: The Planning Foundation

Chapter 1: Your Relationship with ADHD   We begin by learning more about your relationship with ADHD, specifically your mindset around planning. We cover what acceptance looks like, how it can help you become a more confident planner, how limiting beliefs can derail your efforts, and how to challenge them when they arise. You will see how perfectionism sabotages your plans and how to break away from unrealistic standards.

Chapter 2: The ADHD Maze   We explain why planning is much more complex than people realize. We define ADHD and executive functions and talk about which functions challenge planning. Planning with ADHD requires a different set of guidelines to plan more confidently and be flexible enough to adjust when needed.

Chapter 3: The ADHD Time Zone   One of the biggest factors in planning is how ADHD perceives time. Too many people expect themselves to see it the same way as neurotypical brains and do not account for it in their planning, which makes planning very difficult to want to keep doing when the plans are always wrong. We outline time blindness, how it affects you, and what to consider when planning.

Chapter 4: Your ADHD Review   We help you learn more about yourself and your ADHD through various exercises and assessments. You will uncover your values and strengths, learn to track your time and distractions, and better understand habits and patterns of behavior. This information will help you choose the right tools for your workbox and, later, how you decide what to plan and when.

- **Worksheets:** Intentions Exercise; Your Internal Compass; Personal Data Summary; Finding Your Strengths; Wheel of Life Exercise; Track Your Time, Distractions, and Emotions

Part 2: The Planning Workbox

Chapter 5: Step 1: Choosing the Tools   You will assess your current planning system and decide which tools to keep and which to replace. You will outline the purpose of each and how they connect to the whole planning system, along with building out a workflow on how new information will be entered into the workbox.

- **Worksheets:** Planning Tools Evaluation, Workbox Requirements, Your Custom Workbox

Chapter 6: Step 2: Building the Workbox   We walk through the process of setting up your workbox, giving you different ideas and strategies for organizational structure, and giving you guidance if you want to color code categories and how to use a combination of digital and paper tools. We walk through the process of breaking down projects into smaller tasks and getting you started using the workbox as soon as possible.

Chapter 7: Step 3: Maintaining the Workbox   We are talking through the process of workbox maintenance. We cover the details and logistics of the Weekly Focus and Daily Detour sessions. During these sessions, you will be learning a step-by-step process, which is your workflow. The workflow is what maintains your workbox.

- **Worksheet:** Reflections Exercise

Part 3: The Planning Workflow

Chapter 8: Step 1: Capture and Collect The first step of the workflow is to capture and collect your tasks from your various inboxes and enter them into the workbox. From navigating the brain dump to multiple-inbox management, we walk you through the process and how to customize it for yourself.

- **Worksheets:** Inbox List, Brain Dump, Planning Workflow Builder

Chapter 9: Step 2: Updating and Prioritizing Next, we guide you through updating the workbox and provide you with methods for prioritizing your tasks with several strategies and tips along the way. You will come away with an understanding of what is most important for each week.

Chapter 10: Step 3: Intentional Planning In this chapter, we bring everything together, and you will learn what intentional planning means and how much value it can bring to your life. We review the benefits of intentional planning and best practices to make it a strategy you can use when needed. We discuss possible roadblocks and solutions to avoid them. We end the chapter by reviewing your workflow checklists and creating one specific to you. But above all, we hope you are inspired to begin living the life you deserve to live.

- **Worksheets:** Intentional Planning Exercise, Weekly Focus Checklist, Daily Detour Checklist

Chapter 11: Planning for the Future The final chapter covers what to do when you notice your planning system isn't working as well as you planned. It happens, but it's not that scary when you expect it and have a plan to get it back up and running. We end with exploring how you can connect long-term planning to your weekly planning.

- **Worksheet:** Long-Term Planning

Back Matter

Conclusion   With our final thoughts, Nikki shares why joy is an important task to be remembered, and Pete reframes what failure means. Together, we hope you walk away feeling inspired and hopeful about planning the life you want to live.

Appendix   In the appendix, you'll find the worksheets we reference throughout the book. They are organized by chapter, and you can also download them from https://takecontroladhd.com/adhd-book-downloads.

Let's Get Started!

Unapologetically ADHD offers you a framework for planning that is a complete system, one that you can trust. Thank you for choosing this book; it's an honor to write about what we love to talk about on the podcast. Thank you for your time and attention.

Turn the page to begin the journey.

PART

I

The Planning Foundation

WITH ADHD, IT doesn't always feel possible to take control of your time when your mind is racing, time keeps ticking, and the endless to-do list never gets checked off. You always feel behind and never feel like your efforts are good enough. This is an exhausting way to go through life.

What if there was a different way? What if you believed there is more to life than a never-ending to-do list? What if you were able to let go of the shame of having ADHD? What if you stopped apologizing, started advocating for yourself, and lived on your terms?

I love these questions because they challenge us to think differently about planning and time management. We believe planning is about designing a life you love, and some of you may not know what that looks like when it feels like ADHD is always in the way. We hope to change this for you, but before we get to the framework of building a planning system, we have some foundation work that needs to be done first.

Part 1 of the book focuses on your relationship with ADHD. Whether you have a new diagnosis or you've known about your ADHD for most of your life, you have some kind of relationship with it. Chapters 1–4 will help you learn more about yourself and your ADHD and give you valuable information to take with you as you customize a planning system to take control of your time.

1

Your Relationship with ADHD

WHENEVER I START a new coaching group, I have two essential guidelines: one, you do not need to apologize for anything, and two, there is no such thing as being late. Even with the guidelines, I still hear the occasional apology for being late. When coming to an ADHD coaching group, I want people to know there is no need to apologize; they do too much of it in real life. I understand there are circumstances where an apology is needed, but usually, what I witness is a person who is struggling with their ADHD and working very hard to compensate for it. It's exhausting to mask your ADHD.

ADHD Masking

Masking is when a person with ADHD acts in a "socially acceptable" way to fit in and form better connections with those around them (ADDA, 2023). You do everything you can *not* to look like you have ADHD. The pressures of fitting in happen in early childhood; some people are so accustomed to doing this and do such a great job hiding their symptoms that an ADHD diagnosis is often missed (Kosaka, Fujioka, and Jung, 2019).

Masking increases anxiety by worrying about what other people think. It leads to perfectionist tendencies and low self-esteem. It's mentally exhausting to give so much energy to pretend to be someone you're not. People often feel like imposters in their own lives, constantly afraid of people finding out about their ADHD.

Here are a few examples of masking:

- Trying to appear engaged in a conversation by nodding and making eye contact
- Responding with general comments to appear as if you are listening
- Making jokes to cover up what you missed or to smooth over mistakes
- Working overtime to compensate for what you didn't get done during the day
- Having a mindset of always trying and working harder
- Overcomplicating things because you want them to be perfect
- Staying quiet in groups to avoid saying the wrong thing

How much of this sounds familiar to you? When you plan your day, do you consider your ADHD? Imagine if masking was no longer required and you were guided by your own terms when planning your day. How would this affect the way you show up in the world? Keep this in mind as we explore how to make this a reality for you.

ADHD Coaching

When people first come to me, they're hurting and looking for anything to relieve the pain. I see the tears in their eyes, and I hear the cracks in their voices. They are looking for systems and strategies to make life easier, to be more organized, to manage time, and to get more done. They are convinced something is wrong with them, and they want to fix it as soon as possible. I listen to their challenges, and then I share something that sometimes surprises them.

There is not one system or set of strategies that fixes ADHD.

ADHD is not something to *fix*. As the book A *Radical Guide for Women with ADHD* advises, "Only dogs and furniture need fixing" (Solden and Frank, 2019, 7). You are not broken, and you're not a problem to be solved. The goal of ADHD treatment is to make it easier to access more of who you truly are, not to get over who you are

(Solden and Frank, 2019, 6). We have the same intention for this book. The outcome is *not* to get more done in less time, more time, or whatever time you have.

The intention is to understand how ADHD impacts how you plan and make the adjustments needed to be authentically you, not someone you think you *should* be.

In coaching, I work with clients on three pivotal areas simultaneously. This is not a linear agenda. We don't approach these conversations like a checklist because they would never get checked off; it's always a work in progress.

- **First, we are learning and understanding how ADHD shows up for them personally.** This is a blurry line because sometimes it's ADHD, sometimes it could be a symptom of a co-morbid condition like depression or anxiety, and maybe it's just who they are. It's impossible to know for sure, but many people find relief in understanding that what they are experiencing is real and complicated and that they are not alone.
- **Second, we have conversations about what it means to accept ADHD.** Acceptance is not all or nothing. You don't decide one day whether ADHD is accepted or not. It comes and goes, and it can be very subtle. In coaching, we recognize the moments and celebrate them. This, in my opinion, will always be more important than the best ADHD strategy. This is what it means to work with your ADHD instead of against it.
- **Third come the strategies and systems you implement to support ADHD.** If we go straight to number three before we address the first two, we are putting a Band-Aid on a deep cut. They work in the short term, but you will not see lasting change without understanding and accepting ADHD.

This book follows the same approach. The first part explores how ADHD affects you. You will learn about your own ADHD and how to think differently when you plan. With an understanding of ADHD, you can accept where it appears for you. For example, some tasks take longer to do, and that's OK. You can use the strategies and systems you learn to plan realistically that support your ADHD.

What Is Radical Acceptance?

Acceptance is a strange word to understand. The dictionary says it means the action of consenting to receive or undertake something offered. I don't love this definition. I don't think many people with ADHD feel they consented to receive their diagnosis or took it as something being offered. I like this definition of radical acceptance (Hall, 2012):

> *Radical acceptance* means to let go of the need to control, judge, and wish things were different than they are.

Radical acceptance doesn't mean you must like what's happening; it means you no longer resist something you cannot change. Radical acceptance is not a consistent feeling that will come naturally to you. You will have days when you're going to be mad at your ADHD. Be mad. When you feel frustrated, be frustrated.

The key is having enough acceptance to reframe how you see yourself and practice self-compassion. I heard my daughter say she hated herself for getting up late one morning. I said, "Would you tell your best friend you hate her because she slept in?" She didn't answer me.

Planning Tip

Because radical acceptance and self-compassion do not come naturally, it's something to practice. Awareness is the first step toward change. Once you notice, you can begin to coach yourself toward self-compassion rather than self-loathing. Ask yourself, how does the conversation change when you come from a place of radical acceptance? It takes time and several conversations with yourself; with each conversation, you build inner strength and confidence.

Treat yourself the same way you treat someone you love.

Some things are easier to accept than others. Being a few minutes late to a meeting is different than forgetting to attend the meeting. It helps to understand *why* you forgot the appointment. Somehow,

ADHD showed up; maybe you ignored the reminder, maybe it was never set up, maybe you got distracted, and time just passed before you remembered again. This was not an intentional act; it doesn't mean you don't care; you care more than people think you do. It's situations like this where the shame of having ADHD sits. Sure, you feel bad that you forgot, but it goes deeper; you believe you're a horrible human being and should never be trusted.

ADHD is not your fault.

One of my all-time favorite movies is *Good Will Hunting*, especially when Robin Williams hugs Matt Damon, telling him it's not his fault and keeps repeating it until Matt Damon breaks down. (What a powerful moment!) This is our moment, between you and me: ADHD is not your fault. Stop blaming yourself for having ADHD.

Apologizing for a missed meeting makes sense, but you don't need to keep apologizing or overexplaining what happened. Part of acceptance is taking responsibility, but for your own peace of mind, please let it go. It was a mistake. We all make them, and we all can learn from them.

What Radical Acceptance Looks Like

I've had the privilege to witness acceptance in subtle comments from the people I work with every day, and I want to share some of the things they've said to me:

- "I gave myself grace for not completing everything on my to-do list. This month is a challenge, and I just let it be that."
- "For some reason, body doubling [having another person nearby while tackling a task] helps so much. It's like grabbing their compassion when you don't have compassion for yourself."
- "Other people's responses are not within my control."
- "I've been doing the dishes at night and going through my routine in the morning semi-consistently over the last week."
- "I think it's also important to give ourselves credit for being brave and being honest and transparent."
- "I made it to all my Pilates classes this week on time and was told that I am making good improvements and progress."

- "Success is every day trying to do something difficult that has been piling up."
- "Realizing I need to write successes more often for the times I feel tired, discouraged, and inconsistent. It all counts. Today I got out of bed and brushed my teeth."

Coaching Exercise

This exercise is meant to imagine what's possible. First, identify where you are now in your life, and then imagine what's possible with radical acceptance of your ADHD. We will use a bridge metaphor: don't worry about how you cross the bridge. This book has you covered on how; right now, the focus is on what's possible.

Imagine standing before a bridge. This represents who you are right now.

- How do you feel about your diagnosis?
- How do you accommodate your ADHD now in your life?
- How do you advocate for yourself now in supporting your ADHD?
- Describe what acceptance means to you now.

Now, imagine you're on the other side of the bridge. This is you radically accepting your ADHD and living with self-compassion.

- How is your relationship with ADHD?
- How do you feel about your life?
- What do you notice, see, and hear around you?
- How do you accommodate your ADHD on this side of the bridge?
- How are you doing this? What are you doing? Who's with you?
- Describe what acceptance means to you now.

Write as many details as possible and hold this image in your mind. Now, find something that will remind you of this image. This is your reminder of why this journey matters. Maybe it's an inspirational quote, a photo representing how you want to feel, a drawing or painting, or a simple note saying, "You've got this!"

What You Believe Is True

As an ADHD coach, I love to ask questions and then listen. I listen to what is being said and what is not being said. I'm listening for absolute language like *never*, *always*, and *can't*. These beliefs are so ingrained in their minds that many clients don't even realize they said it until it's pointed out.

- "It's never worked before."
- "I get started but can't finish."
- "I could never get that right."
- "I'm always late."

Words matter, and the internal conversations you have directly impact your relationship to ADHD.

If you've decided that you won't ever find a system that works for you, you're right; you are never going to find a system that works for you. If you think you need to find the perfect system for it to work, you will be sadly disappointed each time you continue to try a new one. If you think you're only successful if your plans go exactly as planned, you will always feel like a failure.

Just the word *plan* brings up a variety of emotions; anxiety levels increase and hearts pound faster. A client once told me that her parents used to say, "Failing to plan is planning to fail." I'm sure the intention was good, but if you have ADHD, it can be interpreted in many ways.

- "If planning is hard, I must be stupid."
- "If the plan isn't perfect, it's not good enough."
- "I am destined to fail."

Limiting beliefs protect us from what we fear most, like pain, rejection, discomfort, failure, disappointment, shame, and embarrassment. These are the feelings people with ADHD know all too well. If you don't try, you won't fail. They want you to believe it's not worth trying. In the moment, it feels better not to do anything. Unfortunately, this relief doesn't last long because the guilt and shame come back stronger than ever.

It's time to believe something different.

Challenge Your Limiting Beliefs

Limiting beliefs stop your radical acceptance from shining. Challenging these beliefs means you are questioning their purpose; if they are not there to propel you forward, they don't need to be believed.

Here are a few approaches to challenge your beliefs:

- **What story are you telling yourself right now?** Identify the story (limiting belief). Where is the story coming from? Is this something you've always believed, or is it a more recent belief? What are you afraid of? What is the belief trying to protect you from? Is it serving you? Is it true? What's your proof? What is a different story you could tell that would serve you better?
- **Call it by name.** When you notice the story is not serving you, call it out by name. Separating it from your identity lessens its power over you.

  For example: You missed an appointment today and feel horrible about it. *"I can't believe I did this again, I'm so embarrassed. I'm never going to be trusted."*

  Challenge the belief by saying, *"Hey, LB, I already feel bad about missing the appointment; thank you for trying to protect me from future disappointment, but not being trusted is not an option for me; you can go now. I've got this."* While you're at it, call out the ADHD—"Hey, ADHD, we made a mistake, it's OK, I apologized, the appointment is rescheduled, and this time, I have a reminder set."
- **Flip the script.** This is an extension of changing the story; you are flipping a limiting statement into a statement with possibilities and hope for the future.

  Old script: *"I never have time to plan, and I can't find the right system for me anyway."*

  New script: *"I do have time to plan, and I will find the right system for me."*
- **The What If Approach.** Some limiting beliefs start with *what if*. What if this is the worst task manager ever? What if you asked a different question? What if it's the best task manager ever? Make your *what if* questions about positive outcomes.

This, my friends, is a start to a healthy relationship with your ADHD.

To be fair, limiting beliefs show up when feelings are intense due to ADHD-related emotional dysregulation. This symptom involves difficulty regulating emotions and behaviors and may distort one's perspective (Shaw, Stringaris, Nigg, and Leibenluft, 2014). Listen to your body signals when you are upset. If you notice a tightness in your stomach or blood rushing to your face, whatever it may be, please give yourself space to take a break from the situation to nurture your well-being.

The phrase "This too shall pass" is a helpful mantra, because these overwhelming emotions are temporary.

With time and some distance from the situation, you can challenge the beliefs and process the emotions. Limiting beliefs do not disappear; they're a part of being human; however, they do show up less often.

Coaching Exercise

This exercise is designed to help identify your limiting beliefs and give you the tools to challenge them. You never know when limiting beliefs may show up, and when they do, you want to be ready for it.

Take a few minutes to go through the following exercise:

1. Identify a limiting belief that you have about planning.
   I don't believe I will stick to one system.
2. What is the story about this belief?
   I believe I will get bored or forget about it and be back in the same place as I'm always in.
3. Identify where it came from. When did you first notice?
   It always happens—I've tried so many apps and I have a stack of half-written planners in my office. I've always been bad with time management; it became a problem in middle school.
4. Gather evidence. Is this always true? Think of specific examples.
   It has been true; I've never stuck with a system for longer than a couple of months.

(continued)

(*continued*)

5. Challenge the belief with one of the previous options.
   I have never been taught how to set up a system that works for me. Maybe, if I look at it differently, I will get a different result. Maybe if I wasn't so hard on myself, I could release the shame and feel better about who I am.
6. What is a different story to tell?
   Planning systems have not worked in the past; now I'm approaching it differently to get different results.
7. Write a positive affirmation with *I am*.
   I am going to create a planning system that works great for me. I am going to take control of my time. I am going to be a confident planner.
8. Post your affirmation and review it every day.

Perseverance Is an ADHD Trait

One of the characteristics I admire about folks with ADHD is the ability to persevere, which means to persist in anything undertaken, maintain a purpose despite difficulty, obstacles, or discouragement, and continue steadfastly (Dictionary.com).

You don't give up. No matter how many times you get knocked down and ADHD kicks your butt, you get back up. How do I know this? You're reading this book, and I witness it daily with my clients.

This book is going to bring you face to face with your ADHD, and you are going to be confronted with some hard subjects. They come in the form of P words. (I have no idea why they all start with P, and there will be other words with different letters that will challenge you.)

- Planning
- Perfection
- Prioritizing
- Procrastination

However, as you reframe your relationship with ADHD, new experiences show up, ones that will still make you uncomfortable but in a good way. You notice a silent confidence that starts to find its voice. It comes forward in the way of courage and radical acceptance.

You open yourself up to opportunities and new approaches that support your ADHD and offer compassion, worthiness, love, and laughter.

These experiences build resiliency and the confidence that, no matter what ADHD throws at you, you come back stronger than before.

Perfect Is Not Perfect

You probably know perfectionists, Jordan. Most of the time, they know themselves. They are hard drivers who don't finish a job until it meets their standard of *perfection*, whatever that means. In my experience with perfectionists, perfectionism itself isn't usually the trait these folks celebrate the most about themselves. Great bone structure, bold fashion sense, a palate for exotic spice, and more sit atop that list long before we get to *I'm a raging perfectionist*.

Okay, I recognize hyperbole when I write it, Jordan. Some people *love* their perfectionistic traits. It helps them thrive and succeed in highly competitive fields. Who am I to judge? No one, that's who.

Here's the thing. If there was a Venn diagram that attempted to encapsulate adults with ADHD in one circle and people struggling with the maladaptive tendencies of perfectionism in the other, I contend that the Venn diagram would approach a perfect circle.

Thus is our journey down ADHD Perfectionist Lane. It's a beautiful drive, but don't peek behind the homes there. Every building is a façade on a Hollywood back lot. One good shove and the whole place tumbles backward.

It starts with two dirty words in ADHD circles, so pardon my profanity when I write *overcompensation* and *rejection*.

Living with ADHD is the hamster wheel of the negative feedback cycle. Have you ever been told you haven't been able to focus long enough to get a so-called *easy* task done? Ever been told that your memory, inattention, or impulsivity are symptoms

(continued)

(*continued*)

that cause you to fail over and over again? Of course. Now, have you ever been able to easily let go of those comments as you approach new opportunities to prove yourself?

Nope. Because you have ADHD. Living through those past experiences fuels the overcompensation cycle. We experience what we perceive as past failures, and in an attempt to erase them from the story of our lives, we are driven toward efforts to compensate and thus dodge future criticism at great cost.

"But, Pete," you're saying, "you haven't once said *executive function!*" I know, Jordan. And that's a terrific segue.

See, our ADHD is marked by wildly inconsistent performance in no small part because our executive functioning dial has been busted right off our neurological console. That means we get to have days where we are astounding, days that are written about by bards and told to our children's children. We also have days that are marked by such standards as *barely getting out of bed.* That conditions us to set an expectation of high performance, believing we can do anything any time we set out to do it, and only meeting those standards *some* of the time.

Intermittent reinforcement drives us batty, giving us the benefit of visions of success fractured into pieces by disappointment. The result is a self-image of someone capable of doing hard things if only we could work hard enough to do it *this* time the same as we did it *last* time.

The other switch on our executive function console that's all busted up is the chaos/control function. Because we feel out of control so often, our drive to regain it—to find order in disorder—can fuel perfectionistic tendencies. We have to watch that, Jordan, because if you're anything like me when I push on that control function, I can become downright disagreeable. Accidentally cultivating an atmosphere of contention in an effort to control chaos gets in the way of building relationships of trust and respect with others, and no one wants to solve hard problems with a jerk. I've been a jerk before. I'm sure I'll be a jerk again. I don't like myself when I'm in that space. Being aware and talking about how I am feeling in a given situation with the people who matter to me helps to ground me and return me from the more maladaptive strivings of perfectionism.

Rejection sensitivity is a nontrivial component of perfectionism. Ask yourself: how do you *carry* rejection? For me, it's heavy. The slightest criticism can become an extraordinary weight, dragging me into that dangerous territory of hyper-focus on the worst parts of my identity.

This might normally be the part where I tell you that you should just change your mindset, right? Go ahead and stop doing that thing, Jordan, stop focusing on the bad stuff that brings you down.

But I can't tell you that. Living with ADHD, we know that just telling ourselves to stop doing a thing because it's damaging to our psyche is a fool's game. You felt bad before. You'll feel bad again. *No one feels good all the time.* Such a downer, right? But you can't solve ADHD. You can't cure it. You can't skip with it through a field of sunflowers and butterflies. Anything that you try to do to hide from the fact that you *have* ADHD is a con. And that sucks.

What if, instead, you were to rewire that relationship? What if you were to go to bed tonight with the thought in your head that you are in partnership with your ADHD, that you are a coach working with a different part of you, a player that has different skills than you do?

That part of you, the ADHD player inside you, brings talents that you wouldn't know how to harness on your own. Your job becomes not one of stamping down that part of you, distancing yourself from the player forever. Your job is to nurture them, cultivate them, celebrate their victories, and thoughtfully coach them through their troubles.

As a coach, you would never tell your player to ruminate on mistakes and carry the weight of rejection the way you carry

(*continued*)

(*continued*)

yours. You would ask them to think about what they can learn from the experience, what they can integrate into their game for the future. You would teach them the value of rest, not the painful consequence of fruitless journey toward perfect. You would remind your player that when the coaches of the other teams are yelling at them, shouting them down for foul play, all those barbs are sent from a place of uncertainty in themselves.

Your job is to integrate the value of hard work that is freed from the self-judgment of overcompensation and fear of rejection. The sooner you do that, the sooner you get to feel what it's like to celebrate your accomplishments for the sake of the work you put into them. You can look on a freshly organized kitchen shelf with the joy of your own effort, not the shame of how that shelf might not look perfect in a magazine photo. You can look at a well-earned B on an essay with the knowledge that you learned something new in the writing of it, not the shame of having tickled a mercurial professor's fancy enough to see an A.

Perfection for us is not about producing results that are free of error. Perfection has for too long been about overcompensating for our ADHD experience. It's time to stop that. It's time to turn to the work ahead and recognize the joy of participating in the game of life itself. So you can look at a task list overrun with the dizzying wash of words and checkboxes and not feel overwhelmed, afraid, or anxious.

Rather, you can let your gaze fall to the top of the list and let your player take to the court: *What do I have the opportunity to do next?*

Perfect Is the Worst P Word

"I think my to-do list is like a mix of my 'ideal' self (who I want to be) plus who I think I 'should' be plus hustle culture/societal obligations."

Can you relate to this statement? It came from a client, who is a recovering perfectionist. Fighting the need for everything to be perfect was a daily battle. Perfectionism means second-guessing everything, always wondering if you did it right.

Creating a list around your ideal self and who you think you *should* be is setting yourself up for massive disappointment. It makes you believe you need to live up to impossible standards (Yang, n.d.). If you consider yourself a perfectionist, please reconsider. You will never feel good enough, and this is no way to live.

Absolute thinking and overthinking both play roles in perfectionism.

The ADHD mind tends to overthink every possibility, which makes systems more complicated. This usually happens in task managers where you are deciding the organizational structure. You're not sure how to label your areas and projects because you are thinking of every scenario that may happen, which doesn't actually make anything clearer for you. It makes it more confusing.

Overthinking leads to absolute thinking. Absolute thinking is the same as black-and-white or all-or-nothing thinking. You may not even notice it's happening. You believe you can't start working in the task manager until you have it set up "perfectly," not considering that the only way to know if it works is to practice working in it.

Perfectionism sneaks up on you when you least expect it, and it doesn't serve you. It only makes you feel bad at the end of the day. If you find yourself in this mental trap, here are a few ways to reframe your thinking:

- Change your focus to what's going right. Substitute the negative language with positive affirmations.
- Be your own cheerleader and give yourself credit for your effort and the progress you are making.
- Practice your patience muscle; it takes time to learn new strategies, and things will get easier the more you practice.

Living Through the ADHD Diagnosis

I've worked with hundreds of people with ADHD over several years and I've interviewed several ADHD experts on the podcast, and yet I missed seeing the symptoms in my daughter until she came downstairs one day to tell me she thinks she has ADHD. I asked her why and she told me she was doing homework with a friend, who finished in 20 minutes. It had taken her close to two hours. She decided to take an online ADHD assessment and met several of the qualifications. I took the test with her, and we received the same results.

I asked her more questions and realized I missed many signs. For example, I could always tell when she had been in a room in the house because something was always left behind. Her room and bathroom were always messy, and when she cleaned, it meant shoving clothes under the dressers and the bed. At the time she was a gymnast, and any time we talked to her, she would end up in a handstand. In school, she was supposed to write a book report on a chapter book, either fiction or nonfiction. She asked her teacher if it was possible to do her report on a book of poems (having no idea this was her advocating for herself and asking for an accommodation). The teacher said yes, and it blew us all away. This young lady has a gift; her writing could have been her own poetry book.

I made the appointment with the doctor, and we shared our concerns. We were sent home with the standard forms to fill out. She filled it out, as did her dad and I, and two of her teachers; one of them was the teacher who allowed her to read a poetry book. Her teacher's evaluations were very different from ours. They had glowing things to say about her and did not believe she had "attention" challenges. She was a pleasure to have in class, and her grades were above average.

This was not surprising to me, because she got really good at masking without even knowing it. They could call on her in class, and she would reply with a big smile and some kind of answer, hoping that it made sense, because seconds earlier, she was thinking about her floor routine for the next gymnastics meet.

After the forms were completed, we went back to the doctor, and the doctor said with the results from the teachers, they did not believe she had ADHD. They felt it was more depression and anxiety and wanted to treat this first and then told me that my opinion was biased because of what I do for a living. Let's just say I wasn't accepting this answer, and this doctor is no longer treating my daughter.

I searched for someone in my area to make a formal diagnosis that wasn't just based on her teachers. It took some time and we had to be on a waiting list. But we finally got in, and thankfully this was a completely different experience. He interviewed us together and then separately; there were more forms to fill out, and she did some testing on the computer. And a few weeks later, the diagnosis came back. She has ADHD and there was a recommendation that we watch for depression and anxiety as possible co-morbid conditions.

I share this story to let you know that part of the experiences I explore in this book are from the wonderful people with ADHD with whom I've been able to partner in their journey, and I'm also a mother to an ADHD child who is going through her own journey with ADHD. It is a great honor to walk by her side, and I thank you for allowing us to walk by yours.

Coach's Corner

Thank you for being patient and understanding that we can't go straight to the strategies and the tools. Your relationship with ADHD is where we need to start if we want any of these strategies and tools to work in the long run. Many of the topics from this chapter will come up again in future chapters because they're part of living with ADHD. Limiting beliefs don't disappear because we notice them now. Perfectionism tendencies don't just magically disappear because, I tell you, there is no such thing as a perfect plan.

However, you can depend on your perseverance and radical acceptance to show up more often. There is a great sense of relief when you stop masking and show up in the world as you are, unapologetically ADHD. It's time to embrace life on your own terms.

Chapter Summary

The following are the key points from the chapter:

- There is not one system or set of strategies to fix ADHD.
- ADHD is not something you fix; you are not broken.
- Radical acceptance is what you are striving for.
- Stop blaming yourself for ADHD.
- ADHD is not your fault. Say it as many times as you need to believe it.

- Limiting beliefs are not true and can be challenged.
- Perseverance is one of your greatest strengths.
- Perfect is not perfect and it doesn't exist.

The next chapter explores the ADHD maze and how ADHD and executive functions impact planning. This understanding sheds new insight on how to plan your day and week in a way that supports your ADHD, which makes you a more confident planner.

2

The ADHD Maze

WHEN I TALK to clients about organizing their space, I ask them not to compare themselves to what they see in magazines and TV home shows. Organizing with ADHD has a different set of guidelines. It's not about how pretty a space looks; it's about how it functions. Can you find what you need, when you need it?

Just like organizing space, planning with ADHD is not any different, but for some reason it's much harder to accept. In fact, what I see more often is that ADHD is not a consideration at all. It's mainly based on what they think they *should* do, comparing themselves to a neurotypical brain (brains that do not have ADHD). It's not a fair comparison; the two brains are not wired the same way.

What Is ADHD?

ADHD stands for attention-deficit hyperactivity disorder. It is a neurodevelopment disorder where the brain processes information differently and is challenged with regulating a set of cognitive abilities known as "executive functions" (ADDA, 2024).

Executive functions are a group of complex mental processes and cognitive abilities (such as working memory, impulse inhibition, and reasoning) that control skills (such as organizing tasks, remembering details, managing time, and solving problems) required for goal-directed behavior.

Executive Functions Are Your GPS

Let's say you're taking a road trip to a place you've never been. When I was young, we relied on paper maps, but now we have GPS systems built into our automobiles and our phones. You enter the address of the destination, and you are on your way with a visual map and a magical voice telling you when to turn left and right and what's coming up. When you get there, the magic voice proudly announces *You've arrived at your destination!* Ideally, you had a great trip with little traffic or detours and arrived on time.

Imagine executive functions as your GPS system.

These processes enable planning, focus, memory, and organization. In planning, your destination is the end of your week. You have a list of tasks that need to be completed. But there is a problem. Your GPS has a couple of missing wires and a couple of extra ones. It will give you a plan, but there will be some missed turns and a few more stops than expected.

Your GPS is not broken; it's wired differently.

It still gets you to the destination. Different is not wrong or bad. There are more than one way or two ways to get somewhere.

Executive Functions and Planning

Dr. Russel Barkley, PhD, describes executive function as the cognitive process that organizes thoughts and activities, prioritizes tasks, manages time efficiently, and makes decisions (Barkley, 2019). Executive function skills are the skills that help us establish structures and strategies for managing projects and determine the actions required to move each project forward.

I appreciate this definition because it directly relates to planning. One could even say this is the definition of planning. To plan your day, you need to be able to organize your activities for the day, prioritize tasks, break them down into smaller action steps, and manage your time to get it done.

Here are the executive functions that directly affect planning:

- **Organization:** In planning, you need to be able to organize your projects and break them down into action steps. You can't do this very well if you're not sure where to find the projects and tasks to do. Often the planning gets postponed because you don't know where to start. There's too much to do and the lists are scattered.

- **Prioritization:** Everything feels urgent to the ADHD mind, which makes it challenging to decide what to focus on first. It's this indecision where you do nothing or work whatever is before you. Sometimes expectations are unclear, so you don't know what is most important or you do not have enough information to decide. Emotions often get in the way of how you prioritize, and it's not always the right thing.

- **Time management:** Poor time perception challenges the effectiveness of your planning, not considering ADHD will result in a plan that is not realistic. Procrastination happens for many reasons; one is thinking that tasks won't take as long as they do, so you wait to do them, and now you're working under pressure and blaming your time management skills.

- **Distractions:** Living with internal and external distractions that can be expected and not expected will disrupt the best-intended plans. Interruptions can take you off track from your plan, as can new projects and tasks coming in during the day.

- **Working memory:** Relying on your memory is not a good strategy with ADHD. Reminders are needed to follow through with plans. It's easy to think you will remember to watch the clock for the 2 p.m. meeting, but you get distracted, and now it's 2:30 p.m.

- **Adaptability:** The plan goes as planned or fails; there is no in-between. Having a flexible plan is critical, but it requires you to be able to adjust when necessary. Rigidity in ADHD makes it hard to look for other options, and when emotions are heavy, it makes it even harder to recover.

- **Set shifting:** Otherwise known as task switching, it is the ability to switch focus from one activity to another. In planning, transition time is often not built into schedules. You may not even know this is an issue until you track your day. Planning requires you to work on different things, and when transition time is not built into the schedule, the plan can easily be affected.

- **Emotional regulation:** The ability to manage feelings and impulses. When planning, ADHD emotional dysregulation can lead to avoidance, procrastination, and giving up when frustrated. Feelings of shame can make you shut down and affect your daily plan and how you feel about yourself.

This is why seeing "plan day" makes you want to run in the other direction and do anything but plan your day. It's a lot to process but just because it's hard doesn't mean it's impossible. What if there was a different way to plan? What if you worked under a set of guidelines that supported your ADHD?

Planning Your Day *and* Supporting Your ADHD

The traditional definition of planning is the ability to "think about the future" or mentally anticipate the right way to carry out a task or reach a specific goal (Dicionary.com). The mental process allows us to choose the necessary actions to reach a goal, decide the right order, assign each task to the proper cognitive resources, and establish a plan of action.

Planning is based on foresight, the fundamental capacity for mental time travel (Wikipedia).

Foresight means you can predict the future, and mental time travel means you can use past events to imagine possible scenarios in the future (Dictionary.com). I've never heard of mental time travel; it sounds fantastic, but I question how realistic it is.

- **What if we changed the definition of what it means to plan with ADHD?** When we plan, we predict the future; we plan what we *think* will happen. We make a lot of assumptions and when ADHD is not considered, how realistic can you really expect the plan to be? What if you worked under different guidelines that set you up for success?
- **What if you expected plans to change?** If you expect plans to change, you can adjust your expectations and give yourself permission to change your mind. What if you implemented

boundaries to protect what matters most and be content with rescheduling when needed?

- **What if planning is worth it?** Even if plans only work half the time, isn't this better than not having a plan? Imagine what it feels like to have a trusted system and process that even on the worst ADHD days, you know you will be OK.

What Makes Planning Worth the Time?

If planning with ADHD is so complex, why do it at all? This is a good question if you intend to plan how you always have. But what if you approached planning with a different set of guidelines, ones that support your ADHD?

I want you to find out why it matters, but I also want you to see what to look forward to.

- **Provides structure:** ADHD craves structure. However, it can still have a negative association. Remember, you are in control of your schedule; you design the structure. It's not something to resist if you determine the guidelines.
- **Facilitates intentional work:** Planning allows you to determine priorities rather than acting on whatever is in front of you. The decision has been made, and unless priorities change, your work is intentional. This keeps you more focused during the day.
- **Decreases anxiety:** Planning clarifies when tasks will be done; you don't have to waste your time wondering when it will happen because you have a plan.
- **Creates balance:** Planning lets you control what's scheduled on your calendar. If you want to balance your time differently, this is how you do it. If you want time to do that one thing, plan and make it happen.
- **Builds self-confidence:** You won't be able to do everything you want, but you will be confident that you have a system and process to keep things organized. You'll feel better about your choices and free yourself to be who you are, not who you think you should be.

The ADHD Community

There are several advantages to being a part of an ADHD community, one of them being that you don't need to explain yourself. In every coaching group, I witness a member sharing a story, and at least two heads shake in agreement. It doesn't have to be an elaborate story either. It can be as simple as "I got out of bed today." And the whole group nods; you don't need to say anything more; they get you.

I encourage you to connect with other people with ADHD; it's one of the biggest takeaways people talk about in group coaching and our patron community. It's a special kind of support and understanding you will not receive anywhere else. I remember someone telling us she's so appreciative she can talk about her to-do list with people and not be embarrassed. Until now, she hid her challenges—in other words, masking them, as covered in Chapter 1. People share the hard times with such honesty and courage, *and* what's working to encourage others; it feels good to be the one supporting someone else and not feel like you're always the problem. Every human wants to be validated, seen, and heard; this is what the community stands for. If you haven't found your community, I encourage you to keep looking. There are many opportunities to connect with others with ADHD.

What It Feels Like

When someone asks me what I do for a living, I usually say that I work with adults with ADHD. I don't say I'm an ADHD coach because many people don't know what that means. They imagine me on the sidelines coaching an ADHD team doing some kind of sport. I guess, in a way, that's true; the sport for this book is planning with ADHD. The next comment is something about how they think they have ADHD; they're always distracted. This is annoying, but because I'm a nice person, I usually smile and nod and say something in my mind that's not so nice. The other response is that people are genuinely interested because their lives have been impacted in some way by ADHD. It's not easy to explain to someone what it feels like to have ADHD.

Here are a couple of comments from ADHD experts that explain what ADHD is like:

- "It's a chronic sense of overwhelm. It feels like you're being attacked in all areas of your daily life—like sounds, lights, and sensory things can be overwhelming." Terry Matlen is the author of *Survival Tips for Women with ADHD* (Whitbourne, 2021).
- "Your brain is very powerful. You have a turbo-charged mind—like a Ferrari engine, but the brakes of a bicycle, and I'm the break expert." Dr. Hallowell is the co-author of *ADHD 2.0* (Hallowell and Ratey, 2021).

Here's what a few members of the ADHD community had to say:

- "It's like the mind is a big crossroads, without traffic lights or any other regulations, where thoughts are just driving as they like, and some thoughts and emotions don't even bother if they disturb or hurt; they just pop out."
- "Having ADHD for me means I have a very unrealistic concept and relationship with time, and all things related to time. Also, space, distance, and volume but time is the big one that makes my life so difficult."
- "Having ADHD feels like having a smartphone for a brain with all notifications turned on and there is no 'do not disturb' option to mute them."
- "Having ADHD feels like knowing that I can't explain anything in one or two sentences and that I also struggle to explain things without a word limit."
- "It's hard to know what ADHD feels like when I don't know what 'normal' feels like, but the first thing that comes to mind is how hard I work not to lose things. 'Donna, you would lose your head if it wasn't attached' was a common refrain of my childhood."
- "Time is a thing that you have so much of until you realize you're late, again. Planning? Nah, I'd rather wait until the last possible moment and then miraculously get it all done at the cost of my self-esteem and personal energy."

- "Living with ADHD: a perfect paradox. We fully exhibit the duality of human nature because we *know* that our extremes are temporary, *but* in the present, we can *feel* there will be no end. We are the cat Schrödinger left in the box, and perhaps, as with Pandora, we can give hope to the world by saying, 'I can do hard things' when the world says, 'You can't.'"
- "Super smart and super dumb, all at the same time."

Fishy Behavior

I had a professor in college who introduced me to a concept that has become a guiding principle in my life. Now, I know that people *say* that kind of thing all the time, but hear me out. Once you start thinking about your own daily derring-do this way, I'll just bet you see things a little bit differently, too.

And it all starts with fish.

When was the last time you saw a single fish trucking around the ocean? I'm not talking about the big rigs of the sea, mind you; no sharks or whales here; I'm talking about your basic tuna, herring, maybe your odd anchovy.

Here's the answer: unless that tuna has some sort of death wish, you haven't. You see, there are some basic guidelines that govern the life of a fish and how fish relate to one another.

The first thing you must understand about our tuna friends is that they don't like to swim alone. They don't know why. If you ask, they won't tell you. They are simply attracted to one another such that a lone tuna will find another tuna and then just hang out swimming, nice and close (but not *too* close). If there is a group of tuna, the rule says they'll always try to swim to the middle of the group. The individual tuna is hyper-attuned to overcrowding. When he gets too close to a buddy, our tuna moves a bit out of the way. They're very finicky, the tuna. Get enough of them together, they'll really take you to *school*.

You see what I did there, right? Perfect.

The second guideline is where things get good. See, our fair tuna, now happily swimming in the middle of the school, must always swim in the same direction as the rest of the school. If a tuna to one side turns a bit, our tuna turns, too. And if that rule, which applies to our tuna, also applies to all the tuna in the school, then a single tuna turn will turn the entire troop.

Now, let's explore an example. Let's say our school is swimming along happily when one of them notices a predator like a shark or a killer whale. What happens? The guidelines kick in. The tuna with his eye on our shark—we'll call him Jeff—turns to avoid it. But the tuna next to Jeff may not have seen the shark. All they care about is the second guideline: our job is to keep swimming in the same direction. They turn. This kicks off a cascade of turns that—let's be honest—we puny humans could never match, and it's also why we should always be scared of sharks with tuna around. We will lose that race every time.

See, our guidelines are critical for Jeff and his school of tuna. By swimming in groups and always swimming in the same direction, they are able to avoid predators, adapt to their changing environment, share information with one another, and probably get a hell of an education along the way. Schools of fish are incredible.

Why does this talk of tuna matter to us and our ADHD?

These internal guidelines actually create a new set of *emergent behaviors* for the school that did not exist for Jeff swimming alone. Emergent behaviors can apply to us humans just as well, and it's a great way to discover and cement new routines and systems for your ADHD brain.

In fact, that's a core intention of this book. When we talk about putting new systems in place, we're asking you to think about the guidelines, not a strict set of rules or acronyms. Let's take a simple and ridiculous example of a set of guidelines at home that are likely more relevant than learning to turn like a tuna.

You lose your keys. A lot. Maybe every day. In a typical organizing system, you might try to train yourself to put the keys

(continued)

(*continued*)

in a bowl by your front door every day when you come in the house so they'll be there by the door when you leave again.

For some reason, your expression of ADHD doesn't allow that, and your keys are, once again, in the pantry with the cereal.

As a brief aside, finding keys in the pantry is not the ridiculous part of this example. I find all *kinds* of things in the pantry that don't call for dry goods storage of any sort. There is no shame in that.

If your keys end up in the pantry, maybe that's your first guideline: keys live in the pantry. Always. It's novel enough that your brain might just hold that information for once. But just to be sure, put your wallet and phone in there, too.

"OK, Pete," you're saying. "That's a great idea because it's weird, and my brain likes weird stuff. But what's *emergent* about that?" Great question, Jordan. What if putting your keys in the pantry by the Honey Nut Cheerios drives you to put your phone in the pantry, which ultimately leads you to watch fewer dumb videos on your phone when you should be sound asleep, leading to better sleep, better days, and greater attention in that one meeting you hate, which leads to a promotion? *You could get a promotion because of your pantry keys?* Maybe, Jordan.

Maybe.

I'll settle down. But this is what I'd love for you to take away from this little diversion: our behaviors emerge from the often subconscious systems in place all around us. And you can reverse-engineer them for great benefit. The greatest organizing systems are not systems with prescribed rules and numbered folders. Just like Jeff at school, the best systems offer guidelines that are easy to internalize and allow productivity, organization, or improved planning to *emerge* as a byproduct of those guidelines.

As you read this book, think about how our guidelines might be best interpreted to become your guidelines, simple structures that you can internalize to allow you to make significant changes in your life.

The ADHD Shame Spiral

When something doesn't go as planned, often the first thought is to believe you did something wrong. Pete and I talk about this on the podcast and refer to it as the *ADHD shame spiral*. It's directly related to Rejection Sensitive Dysphoria (RSD), which is one manifestation of emotional dysregulation (Dodson, 2019). It's explained as an intense emotional pain suffered when a person with ADHD receives real or perceived rejection, criticism, or teasing. It leads to negative self-talk, low self-esteem, and never feeling worthy. You may avoid certain social situations to prevent feeling rejected or not applying for a new job because you undervalue your qualifications and assume your application will be rejected. RSD is triggered by an event and isn't something that is always present. After the experience, many are ashamed of their overreactions and fall into what we call the ADHD shame spiral.

Your history with planning and time management has probably caused a few of your own ADHD shame spirals and RSD moments. Being late, missing a deadline, forgetting a task, overestimating what you can do, procrastination, and perfectionism can take a person down the cycle of feeling intense shame and being overwhelmed.

Emotional Distress Syndrome

One of our dear friends is James Ochoa, author of *Focus Forward: Navigating the Storms of Adult ADHD* (Ochoa, 2016). The storms he describes in his book come from the Emotional Distress Syndrome:

> Emotional Distress Syndrome (EDS) is the cumulative effect of the neurological processing differences and behavioral challenges associated with ADHD. It's a chronic state of emotional stress directly related to the struggle to live life with ADHD, a stress that breaks down emotional tolerance, stamina, and the ability to maintain a strong sense of well-being and spiritual health. The chronic, lifelong nature of ADHD-related stress can increase to such a level that it becomes a syndrome akin to post-traumatic stress disorder (PTSD).

An event triggers Rejection Sensitive Dysphoria, but EDS is a chronic state of emotional stress. These moments of intense emotions are part of living with ADHD. They will need to be managed for the rest of your life. If they are not recognized, you continue to spiral, and it will affect every aspect of your life, mentally and physically. These great experts like Dr. Dodson and James Ochoa are sharing an explanation of what's happening. They help you put words to what's happening inside of you. You're not crazy or too sensitive. You feel deeply. These moments pass, and you can weather the storm.

Our wish for this book is to help you create a planning system that you can fall back on after the storm has passed. Instead of looking at these tools as more reminders of disappointment, we hope you can see them as supportive friends that help you put some order to the chaos.

Good Enough Is Fantastic

You have probably heard this before: "It doesn't have to be perfect, just good enough." It sounds good, but what is good enough? How do you know when you get there? Is there an alarm that goes off? Do you get a phone message from the good enough people police that you can stop? And isn't "good enough" kind of bad? Is this your best effort? Do you really want to produce work that is only good enough?

I understand the intention behind the saying. Nothing is perfect; let the ideal go. OK, got it. Where I believe people get hung up on is the relationship between effort and good enough. Do you do less? Do you not try as hard? Does it mean you don't really care?

I don't believe *any* of those things. What I have witnessed are ADHDers who are trying their best, doing more than what's expected, working very hard, and caring very much, maybe too much. It's OK to take the mask off.

Good enough is not only good enough, it's fantastic.

What is your definition of good enough? Sometimes a change of perspective can make a difference and allow you to let go of previous limiting beliefs.

Intention Matters

One of my favorite words is "intention." For me, it means that I've thought about the purpose of doing something, I have a clear reason, and it's important to me that it always comes from a good place.

I remember being struck with imposter syndrome (a psychological occurrence in which people doubt their skills, talents, or accomplishments and have a persistent internalized fear of being exposed as frauds), and I heard Oprah Winfrey talk about intention. She said she always thinks about her intention before deciding to do something. This was an incredible gift for me because it gave me peace of mind and I no longer struggled with imposter syndrome. If I know that my intention behind something I say, write, or create—whatever it is—is coming from a good place, it's OK not to know all the answers. I'm good. Even if someone disagrees or gets mad at me, I know my intentions are good and that's all I can give. I hope to give you some of the same peace I received.

Good enough is *not* less than.

Good enough is doing the best you can with good intentions. Nothing is perfect with planning because we are not fortune tellers and planning is about predicting the future. Even planning 30 minutes from now is still a guess. We assume in 30 minutes, this task will still be the most important to do out of the 20 tasks on the list, and we will have time to do it because nothing will get in the way in the next 30 minutes. Let's sit with this for a moment; I can think of many things that can get in the way; what about you?

Plans change. Tasks take longer. Distractions happen. ADHD shows up. These are not things to avoid; they happen regardless of whether we want them to or not. They are things to adjust and work with. When you plan (even for the next 30 minutes) with your ADHD in mind, and consider the information you know to be true, right now in this moment, you are doing the best you can.

And that my friend, is good enough.

Coach's Corner

ADHD is a much more complex disorder than people realize, especially for those who do not have or understand it. It affects every aspect of your life. I hope this chapter gives you a glimpse of how your brain is wired and explains why planning is complicated. When you see the different steps in planning, it starts to make sense why it's not as simple as one would think. Not considering your ADHD only makes the plans more unreliable because expectations are set too high, and the emotions at stake take you down an ADHD shame spiral. There is no to-do list worth your self-esteem.

Reframing your approach to planning with the mission to support your ADHD allows you to challenge your old beliefs, *and* instead of accepting this is what it is, you open yourself up to new possibilities.

- What if there is another way to define planning?
- What happens if you redefine what success means?
- What if you believe good enough is fantastic?
- What if you plan your day to support your ADHD?

Chapter Summary

The following are the key points from the chapter:

- ADHD has a different set of guidelines for planning.
- Executive functions are the skills required to plan.
- The ADHD shame spiral happens when something doesn't go as planned.
- Fish have amazing structures in place to keep each other safe.
- The definition of planning can change.
- Flexibility can be a part of the plan.
- Good enough is fantastic.

You would think this chapter would be enough to explain why it's so essential to keep ADHD in mind when planning, but wait until you learn about the ADHD Time Zone. Coming up, we explain the complicated relationship ADHD has with time.

3

The ADHD Time Zone

LIVING WITH ADHD means living in the ADHD Time Zone. It's not like any other time zone in the world. It's not always two hours ahead; sometimes it's four hours behind, and sometimes there's no difference; it just passes. Many people in the ADHD world call it *time blindness*. Time blindness is a cognitive condition that causes difficulties in perceiving and managing time, often leading to challenges in punctuality and planning (Pedersen, 2023).

For ADHD, time is less like a straight highway and more like traveling the backroads with road construction and many detours. Minutes feel like hours, and hours feel like minutes, depending on how interesting the drive or podcast you're listening to is. Something grabs your attention, you miss the exit, and now you're lost.

The ADHDer's Heroic Stand Against Time

Jordan, we need to talk about time. This is what happens when I pick up a sword and shield and go to battle against time itself.

We all have the same 24 hours in a day.

How many times have you heard that? I bet you've heard it a lot. I have, too. Even worse, I've *said* it, out *loud*, to *people*. Even as I write that admission, it presents a dose of self-loathing we'll

(continued)

(*continued*)

have to cover later. As a side note, this story comes at a time in my life before I was married to a delightful neurotypical woman who now helps me to usher projects over the finish line when I otherwise drop the ball.

With that, I present "A Trip to IKEA."

By now, I have to assume that purchasing something from global superstore IKEA that you must assemble from parts yourself, guided only by a cartoon globule with a grin, is a universal constant. If you have not made such a purchase, please go out and buy yourself a Billy Bookcase and then come back to this book when it's fully assembled. We'll see you next summer.

The process is a *lot* for my brain. First, there must be a need. That means I must have been aware enough of my own space to notice stacks of books and things gathering around me that require shelving. You know what that's like, right? Because it takes exactly no time for cluttered spaces to render themselves invisible.

So, let's just say for the sake of narrative economy that I do recognize the need. From there, I have to borrow a car that is big enough for the job. Now, I'm telling you *here* that I know I must borrow a car as a second step because I'm doing what we call in the business "burying the joke." So now you know that I know that I should have a car big enough to carry a big Billy Bookcase.

I have a need, I have a car, I go to IKEA. But IKEA is on rails. I walk in, and I'm effectively ushered on tracks through the store. It's a model of efficiency, but I'm confounded by what it means to get off the rails. Are the Billy Bookcases in the living area? The bedroom area? Epic warehouse area? I don't know because my brain doesn't work like that of a Swedish retail architect. Even as I'm writing this now, I can't tell you where the Billy Bookcases are in the store. I have receipts to prove I was there and that somehow, along the way, I also bought a lamp and too many kitchen tea towels. I don't remember where those are in the store either.

At this point, let's take a stab at this exercise from the perspective of me as pretend-neurotypical-brained person. A neurotypical brain probably discovered the need for the Billy Bookcase early one Sunday morning. "Hm, that right there is a mess of clutter and an accident just waiting to happen," they might say. Then they would call their friend Curt, who has a pickup truck, and ask to borrow it for an IKEA trip. Curt, friendly as always, would have said, "Sure! I'll go with you! You'll need a hand carrying the thing, and I could use a few things, too!" Everything is so friendly and easy for the neurotypical and for Curt.

The neurotypical and Curt would find themselves at IKEA before noon and back out of the parking lot with the Billy Bookcase and sundries loaded up by 1 p.m. The Billy Bookcase makes it home. It's on the floor of the space in question. But there is clutter. I bet you know of the clutter. It's the clutter you can't see, the invisible clutter from earlier, which now impedes the actual construction of the Billy Bookcase.

But I clean the clutter because I am a neurotypical hero.

And I build the Billy Bookcase.

And I clean up the construction area.

And I take the cardboard packaging out of the house and deposit it into the recycling bin.

And I place the books formerly stacked about the room into their new home on the Billy Bookcase.

The workspace is ready, and the neurotypical, as if raised speaking the native language used to write the IKEA instruction guides, has the Billy Bookcase built before the sun sets. By dinner, they are standing in the space in a power pose, hands on hips, looking over the new Billy Bookcase with the same mix of pride and awe as Attila the Hun gazing over the Caspian Sea. Theirs is a righteous conquest, assembling a Billy Bookcase, and they have proved victorious.

(*continued*)

(*continued*)

Now, we turn from the land of make-believe to me, the ADHDer, with a brief table of milestones in the acquisition and assembly of the Billy Bookcase:

- Note of need: A Sunday in April
- Considering time: Four days
- Call truck friend: Following weekend (one does not bother Curt on a weekday for something happening at an undetermined point in the future)
- Schedule IKEA trip: The following Sunday
- IKEA trip: The Sunday after that, 8 hours
- Deposit Billy Bookcase at Home: Sunday night
- Assemble Billy Bookcase: The following August, after the kids go back to school, and it's not so busy around the house; all-day event
- Clean area: September 1

- Put books on Billy Bookcase: Oh, wait . . . I never did that.

Let us come back to the adage that we all have the same 24 hours in a day. You see, the neurotypical was able to use those 24 hours for the entire project and likely included a stop for coffee and a plate of Swedish meatballs too. For me, that one measure of 24 hours took five months and, without external intervention, would not be complete to this day. Why?

It's because the ADHD hour isn't shaped like the neurotypical hour. It's more of a blob than a line, and one hour can't be expected to be shaped the same as the last hour, either. If I pretend hard enough, some hours are linear hours, sure.

But it never lasts.

When I'm in an ADHD hour, I find it hard to get out of it. It's as if the clock stretches around me. I can see the end of the hour coming, but I never reach it. I lose time and attention, my focus is fractured, and projects string on for days inside of that one ADHD hour.

The ADHD hour is capricious. It is a trickster. It is prone to outbursts of panic and rage. And from time to time, it disappears completely. When I am asked why I have crafted such a set of guidelines for tracking work and time in my life, it is because time has never behaved with me the way it appears to behave for others.

For my ADHD brain, time is an antagonist.

The neurotypical doesn't have the same 24 hours in the day that I have. They may mark it the same on their clocks and calendars, and for the sake of convenience in conversation and planning, we can all act as if we have the same 24 hours in our days together.

But we, those of us experiencing this book together, know that's not true. Accepting that our hours behave differently is a step toward developing a lifestyle that is resilient to the ADHD hour's whimsy. This is the time zone in which we live. Country to country, city to city, we are inhabitants of the ADHD Time Zone. Once we understand that we don't have the benefit of a stable internal clock, we are free to think about how we relate to the world around us in a new way.

What It's Like to Live in ADHD Time

Anyone reading this book knows it's a confusing place to live. How is it possible to always run 5–10 minutes late everywhere you go and have no grasp of how long it takes to get things done? Feeling confident about planning is challenging when so many things about time do not make sense. There are several reasons why time blindness gets in the way of planning. In the following sections, I highlight the ones I see most.

Estimating Time

The most common complaint I hear from clients is they *can't* estimate how long tasks *should* take. It's a confusing relationship because when things take longer, you feel bad, but when things take less time than you expected, you feel bad for not doing it sooner. It's a time trap when you think you can do one more thing because the one thing doesn't take the 5 minutes you thought it would. It's taken 30 minutes, and now you're late for the next appointment.

The general advice is to double the amount of time you think it takes, and if you have ADHD, you may need to consider three or four times the amount you think. This sounds like great advice, but does anyone really do it?

Giving yourself permission to do fewer things in a day is difficult to accept. When I suggest it to clients, their first reaction is often a strong feeling of resistance. "No, this isn't an option" is usually followed by feelings of already being behind and wasting too much time in their day.

I understand the resistance. However, nothing will change if you continue to do the same thing every day. You will continue to set expectations too high and be disappointed at the end of the day.

There will always be a to-do list, and when one is completed, a new one will appear. So I'm asking you to take a chance and see how it feels to plan your day with realistic expectations, which means planning fewer tasks. Let's replace the shame and always feeling defeated with pride for the work you did and remember that life is more than your to-do list.

It's an unfair question to ask someone with ADHD to estimate how long something will take, especially if it's a new task or one that's not done very often.

You will learn in Chapter 10 that when we talk about intentional planning, the mission in this strategy is not to finish a task; it's to plan when you are working on it. We don't know how many time blocks are needed and it's not worth your time trying to figure it out.

If someone asks you for an estimation, the best answer is that you don't know until you start the work, and you will keep them updated. This way, you're not overpromising and you're keeping the lines of communication open.

Tasks you do regularly are easier to estimate because you can track the "real" time it takes to complete them. You can use this information in your daily and weekly planning and be confident that the time is close enough to being accurate. This supports your ADHD and makes you a more confident planner. We will talk more about this in the next chapter.

Hyper-Focus

Hyper-focus is the intense state of concentration experienced by some people with ADHD (Cootey, 2022). People have difficulty controlling where they focus. Some tasks can be hard to concentrate on, while others can consume them completely.

Is this ability a superpower? I'm not sure. I know many ADHDers who do not like this term. I'm not here to judge if it's good or bad; what's important is that you know what it is and how it affects your planning.

The concept of hyper-focus is the opposite of what you think ADHD is, a distraction issue. Anyone with ADHD knows it's more than a distraction, but it gets confusing how you can focus on one thing so intently that you forget to eat, and now suddenly eight hours have passed. It has to do with interest level. The more engaged you are in the task, the higher the chance that hyper-focus will show up.

Planning for hyper-focus is difficult because you don't know when it may appear. However, there are still a few things you can do to support your ADHD and your planning efforts:

- Identify the tasks and activities that are at higher risk for hyper-focus.
- Schedule activities when they don't compete with priority tasks.
- Set a time limit.
- Use alarms to remind you of the time.
- Set an alarm 15 minutes before the end time to warn you.
- Set an alarm at the end of the task to end it.
- Ask someone to check in with you at the end of the time.

Transitions

You are not alone if you find the transition when switching tasks difficult. Some of this may come from hyper-focus or maybe you found your flow and momentum and do not want to stop doing what you are doing. The formal definition of *transition* is a change or shift from one state, subject, place, or the like to another: a period or phase in which such a change or shift is happening (Webster.com).

There are significant transitions, like moving to a different city, changing jobs, marriage, and/or divorce, and medium transitions, like going on vacation and coming back from vacation. The focus of this book is the more minor transitions like going to and from work, switching tasks, and the time between meetings.

Transitions are not always planned and come as a surprise through distractions and interruptions during the day. This is a lot for the ADHD mind to process; not only can the transitions be annoying, but they carry heavy emotions. However, you can plan for some transitions, and when you do this, it's supporting your ADHD.

Here are a few ways to consider transitions into your weekly and daily planning:

- When planning, ask yourself, *What transitions do I need to plan for today?*
- Create buffer time in the schedule to allow transitions to happen.
- Be intentional about scheduling meetings, avoid anything back-to-back, and give yourself at least a 15-minute grace period.
- During transitions, identify what supports your ADHD—for example, body movement, taking a little walk, doing a few jumping jacks, going outside for a nature break, doing a breathing exercise to calm your nervous system, getting some water and a protein snack.

Over the years, the question has been asked, *How do I return to the work I left behind?* It can feel a little disjointing to leave something you weren't ready to leave, there may be a fear of forgetting where you left off, and now you must start over again. If you feel like you must start over again, I ask you to challenge this because it might be a limiting belief, or ADHD absolute thinking is showing up. Do you really have to start over again? What makes you think that? What other options do you have? To avoid the feeling of starting over, note the progress made and where you left off, and clarify the next step to reenter the project.

Now/Not Now

Any kind of long-term planning is difficult with ADHD because of the executive functions required (Hallowell, 2018). The focus is what's happening now, and because many feel so behind, it's the only thing that matters. The future can wait. This is also where the P word "procrastination" likes to show up, with thoughts like *If it's not due right now, I can wait and do it later*. When you add time estimation being a problem, what you thought you could do later is taking much longer than you expected, creating even more stress.

This book is focused on weekly and daily planning. Long-term planning is a different beast. However, it's important you see how this part of ADHD time blindness impacts planning in general.

Planning Tip

To help you visualize the future, invest in a yearly calendar that you can put on your wall. This way, you can see what day it is now and how many days or weeks are left before a big event or due date.

Time Blindness

When I talk about my relationship with my ADHD, Jordan, I talk about it in terms of the degree of *compromise* that embodies my experience at any given time. I tell you this first so that you'll know a little bit more about me and the language that pops out when I'm talking about my brain. Second, it's because this brief aside should properly set up the direct causal relationship between time and the consumption of cereal.

My memories of high school and time are fuzzy, but talking to my mom about it, we could come up with no real challenges with managing time. My hunch is that this is because I was vastly overcommitted and was forced to change contexts enough that I was dragged from event to event on someone else's

(continued)

(*continued*)

schedule, which most often trumped my own otherwise calami-
tous instincts.

Then I went to college, and things got real. I had a schedule,
sure; it was a list of classes. But—and this is a critical difference
between high school and college—I found myself sitting in a
faraway town on a bed that was too small, staring at an out-and-
proud ADHD roommate, and I had nobody in my life to drag me
around, and tell me what to do.

So I committed my life once again to overcommitting. I
joined the theater club and started auditioning for plays with
gusto. I auditioned for an a cappella group and made it, taking me
into New York City every weekend to busk on the street corners.
I started building computers from scratch.

I started skipping class.

Real talk, Jordan: enrolling at a good school and not going to
class to take advantage of it is the fullest expression of a self-own.
In case you don't know this, not going to class does not actually
reduce academic stress. I was optimistic but ultimately let down
by this. What's more, unlike high school teachers, college
professors do not hunt you down to remind you that assignments
are due or that tests are coming up. Amazingly, they do not appear
to care about nonperforming students in their classes.

I know, right?

This is when I first discovered what it felt like to be compromised. I would visit the music practice rooms to learn a song at
4 p.m. and find myself falling into bed at 2 a.m. I'd start building
out a case for a new PC and have it finished the following day,
forgoing hygiene and diet altogether. And when I was the most
compromised, routines the most unsettled, I made it worse by
hanging out with Sir Charms, aka Lucky the Leprechaun,
longtime mascot of ADHD dietary stalwart Lucky Charms
Cereal.

I came to find out, frustratingly late in life, that this experience
of losing time is what we call time blindness.

You see, my brain does not experience time like you see on a clock. I can look at a clock and watch a sweep secondhand moving in loving circles around the dial all day long. But as soon as I look away, I'm adrift. Time, as they say, is a river. It does not stand still. Also, like a river, it doesn't always move at the same rate.

"Sure," you're saying. "We get it, Pete. It's like watching the clock on the wall of English Lit late on a Friday afternoon. The last class always moves the slowest."

Exactly. You're getting it. When you're doing something you're not connecting to, it feels like time is at a standstill. The river is slowing.

When I am compromised, I lose my connection to time as it passes. When building a computer—something I love dearly—I'll find myself in the rapids of the river of time. I'm focusing on technical details that engage a wonderfully enticing part of my own brain, and I ride those rapids enthusiastically.

But unlike the clock in that high school classroom, the bell never rings.

Unchecked, I'll miss meetings and events. I'll put off the most challenging work to the last minute, counting on adrenaline and hoping to get things done. I'll forget to take care of myself—basic nutrition and hygiene tasks—and resort to the one thing that my distracted brain has internalized for the better part of five decades. *Pete feels better when he's all up on his Lucky Charms.*

Compromised Pete is a kid who has forgotten to eat cereal from a bowl and who sits in front of his desk eating handfuls straight from the box. This Pete is a kid who can build the hell out of that computer. But he does so with his heart pounding out of his chest, oblivious to the world around him.

But the world around him is good, special, and beautiful. That's why the systems outlined in this book are so important. Your ADHD brain is incredible, and it only gets better when reminded that the world outside is better with your ADHD brain thriving in it.

How to Live with Time Blindness

Throughout the book, you will learn how to live with time blindness because it becomes a part of how you support your ADHD when planning. But it's also good to have a set of strategies in place to add to the toolbox.

- Make sure to have plenty of clocks around the house and office. Not just the digital ones but old-fashioned ticking analog clocks. You can never have too many clocks when you have ADHD.
- Use alarms and reminders for transitions and to remind you of when to leave for appointments.
- Ask real people to check in and remind you what time it is.
- Post important reminders in front of you. Out of sight, out of mind is not supporting your ADHD.
- Double-check your calendar during the day to remind you of what's next.
- Schedule buffer time between appointments to allow for distractions, transitions, and anything else that may arise unexpectedly.

The Budget of the Unknown

When I started working on my contributions to this text, Jordan, I had no idea that I would end up stacking it with financial metaphors. Yet here we are, leaning in on a subject that comes straight from our fair financial services friends in the form of the *uncertainty budget*. I'm as stunned as you are, believe me, and so that you will stick around and keep reading, I'll just go ahead and spoil it: this essay is really about impulsivity.

The uncertainty budget is a tool that allows for proper contingency planning to address situations in which you are reckoning with risk or an inherent margin of error that may affect the outcome of a project or task. For the spreadsheet-minded out there, once you have that margin of error, you can determine the extra resources that you might need to assign to the riskier line items to account for its relative uncertainty. It's an incredibly useful process, building an uncertainty budget, and now that you know about it, go forth and budget with glee.

I have lunch every Wednesday with my dear friend Curt (yes, *that* Curt, the one with the truck). Curt is a software architect for a great big publishing conglomerate and often tells me about the work of the organization because I'm a nerd for org charts. Curt said something to me last week that got me scratching my ADHD brain.

A developer who works with Curt offered a choice of tools for a project. One of the tools was familiar to the organization, while the other was new and untested but offered a number of shiny upgrades. There was an imbalance of internal expertise between the two.

I'm a new-shiny guy myself, so I was a bit confused to hear Curt tell me that he and the senior developers had blackballed the new tech. Why, Curt, why? Paraphrasing, I said something to the tune of "Curt, you blithering moron! Why would you choose the old and broken tool when you have so much new to learn about this fancy and clearly superior one?"

"We have a budget for unknowns," he told me. "There are other elements of this project we don't completely understand. We do understand the current tool." Then I'm sure he said something like, "Peter, you ignorant boob, why would we want to replace certainty with uncertainty around a tool we already know?"

Sometimes, I imagine my relationship with Curt as one between Victorian gentlemen about to engage in fisticuffs.

As soon as I trigger this line of inquiry in my mind, I'm met with a list of events in which I have replaced the known with the unknown with absolutely no forethought or consideration for the implications of those decisions. The foundation for those decisions sits in my fireworks brain, the hyperactive part of me

(continued)

(*continued*)

that no one can see but is the driving force behind the dead-eyed pretend attentiveness that overtakes me from time to time.

I replace the known with the unknown because I allow the impulsive ADHD parts of me to dare me to do it. Sometimes, it pays off.

Because I'm crafty. And maybe a little clever.

Most of the time, though, I get caught in the vortex of lost time, surrounded by rogue components of computers in disarray, or find myself floating atop a flood of emails, wondering why I disappeared suddenly. This is what happens when I forget to attend to the budget of the unknown before I act.

Of the ADHDers I know, our experience of ADHD is wildly unique save for one common skill: we tell amazing stories. This skill likely makes me more resilient than I deserve to be because the lure of the new and the untested is strong against my frail restraint. The exhilaration of beginning new things is vastly more potent than the drab murmur of the *ongoing*.

The budget of the unknown is all about the amazing stories and rationalizations I use in service of my prior impulsive behaviors.

Because our experiences are so unique, Jordan, I don't have a great answer for this save one. I don't think you're going to like it, but I'm going to tell you anyway because it's helped me more than just about any other strategy.

Introduce more friction.

It's crazy since just about everything I preach is about reducing friction so that you can do what you need to do before distraction takes hold. That's my *whole thing*. In this case, friction serves an important function: it slows me down.

When I slow down, I don't buy new computers once a year. When I slow down, I don't visit a new restaurant every other night. When I slow down, I offer my more stable tendencies a chance to catch up to the fireworks brain and speak calmly, clearly, and patiently about how I'm really fine right now and don't need the new gear or another restaurant.

In fact, tomorrow morning, a new computer is going on sale that Fireworks Brain Pete really wants to order. At 5 a.m., I could push a few buttons on my phone and have it delivered.

But what if I put my phone in the living room tonight? What if I introduce that much friction so that I'm forced to stand, get out of bed, and shake the sleep from my head? What if I have an additional 30 seconds between my bedroom and the living room to think about whether I need to introduce this new thing into my life before I know everything about it and the disruptive impact it could have on my work?

That's friction. That slight resistance is insignificant to some, yet for me it is a barricade between impulse and action. A humble speed bump on the road of best intentions, allowing space to weigh the hidden costs of my capricious desires. But it's not about limitation.

As a management tool, the uncertainty budget itself isn't about constraining a project. It's about recognizing that choices have to be made—change happens—and that we should be prepared. Just so, a personal budget of the unknown isn't about telling you that you can't do the things you want to do. In fact, it's the exact opposite. It's a framework for you to think about what lies ahead to make decisions so you'll be ready to act no matter what happens. My budget of the unknown isn't about constraining me, but readying me for exciting decisions I'll get to make later.

It asks only this: first, *reflect*. The rest unfurls from there.

Coach's Corner

Once you understand the ADHD Time Zone and how it impacts you personally, many planning "failures" begin to make sense. Working harder and pushing yourself to do more is not the answer. Planning without considering your ADHD is not setting you up for success; however, when you do consider ADHD, your plans are more resilient to changes, and you no longer take the change of plans as a personal flaw.

I worked with a client who told me her goal was not to have an alarm to remind her to pick up her kids from school. She felt like she should just know the time and not have to rely on an alarm. I feel many people reading this book have had the same thought: *I should just be able to do this without [fill in the blank].* I explained to her that needing an alarm was not a bad thing. Would she expect me not to wear my glasses because I *should* have eyes that work without them? I wear glasses so I can see clearly. She uses an alarm to make sure she leaves the house on time. There is no shame in needing tools and systems to remind you of the time or any other challenge you may face. Let's make life easier, not harder, because of what you think you "should" be doing and do what is right for you with no apologies.

Take a moment to think about the following questions:

- How does the ADHD Time Zone impact you personally?
- What limiting beliefs do you hold about time and ADHD?
- How will this information help you as you create a planning system?
- What if you accept that things take longer, and that's OK?
- What if you stopped comparing yourself to others?
- What if you focused on what is right for you?
- How do your previous responses affect your future planning?

Chapter Summary

The following are the key points from the chapter:

- The ADHD Time Zone is like no other.
- Time blindness is a cognitive condition that causes difficulty perceiving and managing time.
- How fast or slow time passes is largely affected by your engagement in the task.
- For someone with ADHD, 24 hours is not the same as it is for others.

- Time blindness affects time estimation, hyper-focus, transitions, and long-term planning.
- Time blindness needs to be considered when planning.

The ADHD Time Zone certainly impacts how you spend your day; even with the best intentions, time blindness will blind you, and you can't see anything but a bright, shiny light. Coming up in the next chapter is a collection of exercises and assessments to help you uncover how ADHD impacts you specifically. When you have this data about yourself, you begin to plan more efficiently and keep supporting your ADHD.

4

Your ADHD Review

WHEN I SEE people working against their ADHD, it's usually coming from a place of "I should." It shouldn't take this long. I should be able to plan. I should know how to be on time. I should know better. I should have done this. I should all day long. Should is like a cousin of comparing. Who is setting the standard to make it a should? It comes from a place of perfection, comparison, and limiting beliefs.

This *should* for planning is a slippery slope because if it is your standard, you will most likely go down the slope too fast and crash into the people at the bottom of the hill. For some reason, we believe we *should* compare ourselves to others when setting up daily expectations. Then guess what happens? It's a cycle of constant disappointment and repeated frustration. This may be all you know, so I want to open the door for you to do something different.

Let's look inward. Imagine creating a plan that is flexible and resilient to change, one that brings you grace and compassion when ADHD decides to show up. It sounds good to me, so let's figure out how to get started!

Coaching Exercises and Assessments

Much of this chapter includes coaching exercises and assessments to uncover who you are and prepare you to choose the right planning tools for your workbox in Part 2. When was the last time you thought

61

about your values or strengths? Or consider how the ADHD Time Zone affects you. Instead of *should*, what do you really know about your habits and natural patterns during the day? These are the things you will uncover; by completing the exercises in this chapter, you will gain valuable insight into your natural tendencies, habits, distractions, motivators, and preferences on how you like to get things done. This insight is so important when it comes to planning and supporting your ADHD.

Until now, you've been trying to achieve some ideal in your mind that isn't the real version of you. This is no longer the case.

What Do You Want?

You bought this book for a reason. Looking at my own bookshelf, I'm guessing this is also not the only book you have about ADHD, time management, or self-help. I love the feeling of bringing a book home; it's filled with promise and opportunity. They also tend to stay on the bookshelf unread. For all the books still on the bookshelf that have never been read, don't worry; I still have hope for us. We will meet someday. For some of you, this will be that book, and I'm good with that because the opportunity awaits you patiently. We are here when you're ready.

For those who are ready now, this is what I want for you: clarity of intention.

My Intention Exercise

This exercise is meant for creating your mission statement for this book. Use the "Intentions Exercise" worksheet (**Worksheet 1** in the appendix) to answer the following three questions with two to three words, and then combine the words into 1–2 sentences to create your mission statement.

Example:

- What do you want? Time, Peace
- Why do you want it? Enjoy life
- How will you get it? Read and implement

Mission Statement:

> I want to have control over my time because I believe it will help me achieve peace and happiness in life. To achieve this goal, I plan to read a book that outlines a process for creating a personalized system that works best for me.

Now, it's your turn. What do you want?

Your Internal Compass Exercise

In conducting this exercise, I have always found it helpful to check in with myself. Am I living a life that is true to my values? The intention is certainly to do so, but sometimes everyday ordinary life happens, and we forget to make time for things that matter most to us. And isn't one of the reasons we want to plan because we want to take control of our schedules? If it's been a while since you've done a value check, this exercise is for you.

We have provided you with the "Your Internal Compass" worksheet with several personal values to choose from (**Worksheet 2** in the appendix). Circle each one that feels intuitively most important to you. Narrow it down to your five top values. In doing so, look for similar values and compare them to each other, choose one, or think of a different way to describe both values in a different word. For example, friends and family could be personal relationships. Keep going through the words until you get to your top five.

Then enter the values onto your "Personal Data Summary" worksheet (**Worksheet 3** in the appendix). With these clearly identified, you can reflect on how you currently spend your time and energy each week. Are your activities truly aligning with what matters most to you? This values exercise is a helpful checkpoint to ensure you're living according to your true priorities; if not, think about ways to start doing so.

Identifying Your Strengths

In case you need to hear this right now, you are so much more than your ADHD. You are a whole person with challenges and strengths.

Those strengths need to be identified and celebrated. We get caught up focusing only on what's going wrong, and we ignore what's going right.

Unfortunately, when I ask my clients about their strengths, many people have difficulty answering. Their self-esteem has been so beaten down that they stop trusting when things go well. They believe it's a rare occurrence and don't believe it deserves to be recognized. Even worse, what if people expect this from you going forward? How are you going to make this happen again? If you're not sure what I'm talking about, it's the fear that comes from succeeding. This is just one more example of how limiting beliefs get in the way of believing in yourself.

Identifying and using your strengths builds confidence and courage to discover what you are capable of, which results in new memories (Aluise, 2021). Memories of feeling good and proud of your accomplishments, trusting yourself, and believing good things are meant to happen to you—that's not a coincidence. These are the memories that challenge old limiting beliefs that are trying to tell you something different.

Trust yourself and believe good things are meant to happen to you; it's not a coincidence.

Please use the "Finding Your Strengths" worksheet (**Worksheet 4** in the appendix) to identify your strengths. Filling out the assessment and asking other people what they think gives new insight and, I hope, awareness of where you shine. Once you have completed the exercises, write your top five strengths in the "Personal Data Summary" worksheet (Worksheet 3).

The most rewarding moments in my work with clients are not focused on the workbox we created together but rather when I hear them celebrating their successes and acknowledging a shift in their mindset. It's truly inspiring to see them giving themselves grace, advocating for their needs, and recognizing their strengths, which they use daily. They accept the challenges they face and adapt accordingly.

This is what I wish for you.

Starting a Success Journal

It's important to take note of your successes and when you have used your strengths, but relying on your memory alone may not be enough. That's where a Success Journal comes in handy. You can name it anything you like if the word "success" doesn't resonate with you. Simply jot down your achievements in the journal whenever you notice something good and refer to it for inspiration or to challenge a limiting belief. This journal serves as proof that you can achieve great things.

Knowing your strengths is essential in all areas of your life, including planning. Remember where your strengths shine and where you may need to delegate tasks when working with others. Focusing on your strengths will boost your self-confidence and reinforce that you make good decisions.

This positive mindset is contagious and empowering.

How Do You Spend Your Time Now?

The previous exercises are valuable because they give us insight into our wants and values and help us remember our strengths. The following exercises focus on how you spend your time. If you want more balance in your life and more time to do what matters most, these exercises are the first step toward finding your answers.

Wheel of Life Exercise

The "Wheel of Life" worksheet (**Worksheet 5** in the appendix) is a popular self-assessment tool that promotes reflection on the different areas of your life. Figure 4.1 shows a sample.

Wheel of Life Exercise

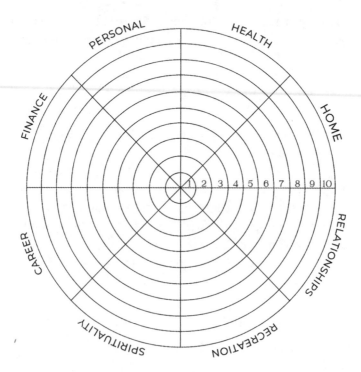

Figure 4.1   "Wheel of Life" sample.

Here is an explanation of each area's meaning; you can change the meaning to match what best fits you:

- **Personal:** Includes education, skills, hobbies, and interests
- **Health:** Includes physical and mental health, diet, exercise, medical care, and wellness
- **Home:** Includes your living environment, household chores, home ownership, and projects
- **Relationships:** Includes family, spouse/partner, friends, co-workers, and so on
- **Recreation:** Includes relaxation, joy, and entertainment—your hobbies, sports, and vacations

- **Spirituality:** Includes your religious, spiritual, or philosophical beliefs and practices
- **Career:** Includes your current job, business, school, and volunteer work
- **Finance:** Includes income, savings, spending habits, and financial goals

On the worksheet (Worksheet 5), you will assess how much attention you give each area. On a scale of 1–10, 1 represents spending no time in this area, and 10 represents all your time there. So, for example, if you think that you spend 90% of your time on your career, then put your career ranking as 9.

As part of the worksheet, there are reflection questions to consider once you've completed the Wheel of Life. These questions will prompt you to think about what areas in your life need your attention. Doing these exercises provides insight into how you're balancing your time. Sometimes, it's not what we want to see or even expect. Even though it may feel bad, it's good information to have because now you are more aware and can start to make changes in how you use your time. If you like, set some intentions for the next 3, 6, and 12 months. Set up reminders to return and do the exercise to notice what changes you've been able to accomplish.

Decide the key takeaways from the Wheel of Life exercise and write them in your "Personal Data Summary" worksheet for later review (Worksheet 3).

Tracking Time, Distractions, and Emotions

The "Track Your Time, Distractions, and Emotions" worksheet (**Worksheet 6** in the appendix) is based on tracking your time. Imagine yourself as an investigator, tracking your daily activities, distractions, and emotions.

Please go into the exercises with a mindset of curiosity and not judgment.

As soon as you hear the little voice saying something like "It shouldn't take this long," please stop for a moment and give yourself grace and celebrate the fact, that right now, you are doing something for yourself that will ultimately make your life better. If you see something you don't like, that's OK; now you have an opportunity to do something different, or better yet, accept this as a part of your ADHD and something you may need to accommodate for.

We are *not* looking for ways to find out where you can be more productive and do more in less time.

This is *not* our mission. Our mission is to learn more about how you use your time now and what your natural habits and preferences are for moving throughout your day. The personal data you collect will be reviewed and considered as you create a planning system tailored just for you.

The planning framework you are learning in this book is based on supporting your ADHD. It's not about getting more done in an hour; it's about being intentional in what you do during that hour.

This is what you need to know before the tracking:

- Track for at least five to seven days. You want to get enough information to notice patterns and habits.
- The tracking does not have to be perfect. If you forget, track it tomorrow.
- Use our worksheets for tracking or use a digital time-tracking app. If you use something different, please be sure you complete the "Personal Data Summary" worksheet (Worksheet 3), because this will be your cheat sheet to use as you build your planning system.
- Pay close attention to tasks you do regularly; when you track the time, you get the real time it takes, and you can use this information later during your Weekly Focus sessions (Chapter 6).
- Don't do anything different just because you are tracking your time. Only you will see this information, and it's too valuable; don't alter the results.

This personal data is pivotal when it comes to planning with ADHD. If you ever wonder how the hours go by and why some tasks never get done, this data may give you those answers and much more. It is incredibly insightful because what you think takes 5 minutes may really take 15 minutes, and the 10-minute difference could be why you're always running late.

Tracking your activities during the day and the time it takes to complete certain tasks will give you concrete evidence of your daily activities, and I'm willing to bet you do more than you think.

Tracking Distractions

When working with the ADHD community, you can imagine that dealing with distractions comes up in many of my conversations—it's in the title of the diagnosis. However, it's still frustrating when they constantly get in the way.

To understand distractions, we need to know where they come from. From there, you can decide which ones you control and which you don't. You can eliminate the ones you have control over and plan for the ones you don't by adding buffer time to your schedule. You will learn more about this concept in Chapter 10.

When tracking distractions, document external distractions like interruptions, the phone, email, and the light buzzing in the office that you can't stop focusing on. However, you should also notice the internal distractions when you daydream or think about the morning meeting and wonder whether you said the right thing.

Be curious about what patterns you notice. For example, do certain distractions happen daily at the same time, or is it completely random? How much time do you spend reading the news or scrolling social media?

After you complete the tracking, take time to analyze your findings and consider how you want to handle these distractions in the future.

Tracking Emotions

Tracking your emotions gives you information about energy patterns, how you feel about specific tasks, and how you feel about certain activities or working with certain people.

Often, avoided tasks have some kind of emotional component, such as shame and/or embarrassment. The awareness of how you feel about specific tasks is helpful because there is more to work through than just the task's action.

Identifying the feeling is the first step; the next is to think about ways to get the task done even with the uncomfortable feelings it brings up for you. Because many ADHDers are verbal processors, it can help to talk to someone else to get the perspective of someone not emotionally invested in the task.

For the "Personal Data Summary" worksheet (Worksheet 3), write down your top three takeaways or insights from each exercise.

Reviewing the "Personal Data Summary" Worksheet

If you have not completed the "Personal Data Summary" (Worksheet 3) after you completed each exercise, now is the time to do it. Review each exercise and write down the key points you want to remember. This cheat sheet is a resource to remind you of your intentions for reading this book, your strengths, values, and where you want to see changes in your life. As you begin to build your planning system, refer back to the summary sheet for personal preferences and how ADHD impacts you. The last page is for any additional notes you feel will be necessary to consider in the future.

Coach's Corner

These exercises are always enlightening in both positive and negative ways. They can be positive because most people realize they do much more in a day than they give themselves credit for. They also come face to face with the number of decisions that need to be made on any given day when it comes to planning and realize there really isn't enough time to do everything. I hope this realization comes with a sprinkle of radical acceptance (Chapter 1), understanding that this is not their fault; there is simply not enough time.

I hope you find the exercises insightful and reflect on them with curiosity, not judgment. You have no reason to apologize for ADHD, any more than I need to apologize for wearing glasses. Please acknowledge your courage to dig deeper and learn more about yourself and your perseverance in continuing to show up and do the work. It matters. You matter.

Chapter Summary

The following are the key points from the chapter:

- Identify your values and celebrate them.
- Identify your strengths and celebrate them.
- Rank the different areas in your life.
- Reflect on the balance of how you use your time.
- Track your time, distractions, and emotions.
- Complete the "Personal Data Summary" worksheet.
- Be thinking about how this information can help you.

Congratulations on finishing Part 1 of the book. You are ready, my friend, to take everything you learned and begin the journey of building a customized, flexible, resilient, planning system just for you! This is exciting—let's go.

PART

II

The Planning Workbox

CONGRATULATIONS ON WORKING through the foundation work. Understanding how ADHD impacts planning and collecting personal data (Chapter 4) gives you a different level of awareness. As you move into the next part of this book and begin to build your planning system, your focus will be on making decisions based on how it supports your ADHD.

The next three chapters focus on the three steps of building your planning workbox.

In step 1, you will select the planning tools for your workbox, which consists of a calendar, task manager, and other essential planning tools to complete the system.

In step 2, we explore different possibilities for setting up these tools and efficiently organizing your projects and tasks.

In step 3, we will discuss how to sustain these systems, preparing you for the last part of the book, where you create your planning workflow.

Let's get started!

5

Step 1: Choosing the Tools

THE NEW YEAR is coming, and you see an advertisement for an ADHD planner, thinking *This is it! This is what's going to keep me organized!* The planner asks for your top three priorities for the day. What, three? You can think of at least 20 things that must be done ASAP. Frustrated, you think, *I will figure this out later; I have things to do!*

Later, you're listening to *Taking Control: The ADHD Podcast*, and Pete mentions the name of his task manager. "Well, if Pete is using, it must be ADHD-friendly," you think. "I'm downloading it today." You start the free trial, but after a couple of weeks, it disappears. Really, it's like it never existed. You don't know why you stopped using it, you just did.

Does this sound familiar?

When I ask clients to share what systems they use for planning, they answer with a laugh, smirk, cry, or look at me like I just asked a question in a foreign language. *What system?* This chapter intends for you to answer this question with no confusion or tears.

This chapter is all about choosing the right planning tools for *you*.

Is the Tool to Blame?

If you can relate to the previous story, you are not alone. It's natural to blame the system and to assume that if you had a different one, you might get different results. However, you don't get different results; the pattern continues, and nothing really changes except the tool. Is the tool to blame, or is it something else? You may be thinking, nope, I know it's not the tool; it's me. I'm the problem, but I will still look for something different because you just never know.

Before you walk into the same pattern as before, let's pause for a moment and investigate what's really going on. As good as it may sound to start fresh, it may not be the best use of your time.

I am often asked my opinion about whether I think it's the tool or something else, and the conversation usually goes something like this:

Me: What's going on?
Client: My system isn't working; I stopped using it.
Me: What's getting in your way?
Client: I don't want to see the overdue tasks. The list is too long, and nothing is getting done. It was too overwhelming to look at it, so I stopped looking at it.
Me: What are you using instead?
Client: I started a new list.
Me: How is this working?
Client: [pause] I haven't looked at it for months.

To summarize, the client questions whether they have the right task manager and wonders if it's time to get a new one. The challenges include the task list being too long, nothing getting done, and feeling overwhelmed just looking at it. They avoid the list because they do not want to see the late tasks. They started a new list, but it's not working; they haven't looked at that for months.

We need more information to make it a fair assessment of the task manager:

- **Is it the task manager's fault for having a long list?** Yes and no. The client entered the tasks into the system, so the long list comes from the client; however, does the client like the layout of the tool? There could be some friction from the initial setup, and they don't like how the tool functions.
- **Is it the task manager's fault the tasks are not getting done?** No, the task manager only tells you what you told it to tell you.

- **Is it the task manager's fault it's overwhelming to look at?** Yes and no. The list is long and overdue. We understand this is coming from the user, but we also must consider the initial setup and if you like the layout and user ability of the tool.

Starting a new list in the same task manager wasn't the solution because it ended up in the same status as the other list: unused and abandoned, like the many planners and task manager apps you've collected over the years.

There is a difference between a tool not working because you don't like its format or functionality and the user not using the tool. This is not to blame you or make you feel bad because planners haven't been consistent for you. I hope it releases some stress of always looking for the perfect tool.

What if you learned a new way to use your task manager?

Planning Tip

When task lists are getting long and few tasks are getting done, this is more likely an ADHD symptom rather than a tool issue. Getting started on tasks requires using executive functions. I recommend looking for strategies to help you get started before adopting a new task manager.

Here are three of my favorite tips:

- Practice intentional planning (Chapter 10). Planning when a task will be completed increases the chance of it being done. "Someday" rarely comes unless you plan it.
- Add accountability to your intentional planning, and your chances of completion just doubled. These two strategies together are like magic. Tell someone what you need to do and when you are doing it and ask them to follow up with you.
- Do something fun before the dreaded task. This increases your dopamine and will put you in a good mood.

Do Your Tools Stay or Go?

Now it's time for you to do your own investigating. Let's look at your tools and decide which ones stay and which ones go. Use the "Planning Tools Evaluation" worksheet (**Worksheet 7** in the appendix) to do the following:

- **Make a list of your current planning tools.** Include anything that helps you manage your time—for example, calendars, apps, planners, and/or notebooks. Is there anything missing that you wish you had?
- **Evaluate your calendar.** If you use more than one, state the purpose of each. Explain how you use the calendar. Is it only for appointments? Do you have tasks on your calendar? Do you practice intentional planning, and if so, how? Do you share the calendar with others? Do others have access to add appointments for you? What works? What doesn't? How does it support or not support your ADHD? Is there anything it doesn't do that you need?
- **Evaluate how you currently organize projects and tasks.** List all the different places you find yourself writing down tasks—for example, digital task managers, paper planners, bullet journals, notebooks, notes or reminder apps, digital routine trackers, calendars, sticky notes, and/or the back of envelopes. How is your current system working? What's not working? If it did work for even a period, what did you like about it? What is your process when a new project or task comes in? Do you need to share it with other people? Do others have access to it? How does it support or not support your ADHD?
- **Analyze and decide.** Finally, use the information you gathered to decide which tools to keep and which to replace. If you're unsure, keep them for now; you will know later how they fit into the system. Learning and setting up new planning tools takes time, and the decision sometimes depends on how much time is available.

Figure 5.1 shows an example of the "Planning Tools Evaluation" worksheet.

Planning Tools Evaluation

List your current workbox and other tools you use for planning. Evaluate how the tool is working for you and if you would like to keep it or find a replacement.

Planning Tools	Reflection Notes	Yes or No
Google Calendar	Works well. No changes needed.	Yes
Things 3	I like the format but it doesn't allow sharing, I need to share the projects with others. Want to start over with something new.	No
Notebooks	I use these to write quick notes, but there are too many of them. I can't find what I need. I want to keep the idea but be more mindful of how I use them.	Yes
Sticky Notes	Always good for quick reminders. I need to work on getting the information into the workbox.	Yes
Reminders App	I use this every once in a while, but it's not consistent and I always forget about it.	No

Figure 5.1   Sample "Planning Tools Evaluation" worksheet.

The Best Tools for ADHD

Some of you may expect a beautifully drafted list of Pete and Nikki's recommendations for the best ADHD calendars, planners, and apps. This isn't going to happen, but with good reason. I hope you believe me when I tell you the tools do not matter as much as you might think. However, if you've gotten this far in this book, this probably isn't that surprising.

Any tool can potentially work for someone with ADHD.

Think of it this way: just because I have the best treadmill in my room doesn't mean I'm running a marathon. The best hammer on the market doesn't make me a carpenter. The best ADHD planner doesn't make any of us time management experts.

There Are So Many Options!

In my experience, I've seen a range of systems. I've seen complex systems I can barely comprehend. I've seen a simple system comprised of no more than a clipboard and a few pieces of notebook paper. I've seen whiteboards hung up on dorm walls with a to-do list for the week. I've seen notecards used as a daily to-do list placed in a back pocket, never to be lost. I've seen several digital task managers work for clients, and I've seen a combination of both digital and paper tools work together. No matter how simple or complicated any given system is, whether I can understand what's going on in it or not, what matters most is that the people who count on those systems understand them. The same holds true for you.

There are many options for planning tools, and boy, do they ever make big promises. They want you to believe this calendar or planner will manage your time and allow you to do more in less time. This promise is a lie. It's simply not true. *You* manage your time, and if you want to do more in less time, you may not be reading the right book.

The intention is not to change how you work, it's to understand it and learn ways to accommodate your ADHD.

Planning Tip

To decrease the number of tools to review, ask others with ADHD what systems they use and what they like and don't like. Remember, everyone is different, so if you come across something that isn't right for you, it's okay. Keep searching.

Which Features Matter?

The features that matter most are the ones that support your ADHD. Now is the time to bring out your "Personal Data Summary" worksheet

(Worksheet 3). This data will help guide you in making decisions based on your natural habits and preferences. For the ADHD mind, it's important to have engaging tools that you like to use. Paper planners have the advantage of creativity, but you can also dress up a digital system with color and emojis to break up the text.

By the end of the chapter, you will have a list of your tools, their purpose, and how they connect with one another to create a complete planning system.

Digital or Paper?

Each platform has pros and cons. The benefits of digital tools include easy access from anywhere with internet access, easy sharing, reminders and notifications, flexibility, customization, and data protection in the cloud. The disadvantages include not being as tangible or visual, more distractions, security risks, cost, and a learning curve.

The benefit of a paper planner is that it's a tangible object and visual outline of time, presents less distraction, the physical action of writing is helpful to remember, and they can be prettier and more creative than digital options. Paper planners are harder to share with others, more labor intensive with maintenance, have limited space to write, and are usually not customizable; and if they get lost, all the information is lost.

How to Use Both

The most common option I've seen with ADHD clients is to combine both formats. Digital systems are great for project management and breaking projects down into smaller, actionable tasks. You can set due dates, alarms, and reminders and write the details of a project all in one place and not constrained by space limitations. If your handwriting isn't great (like mine), it's clean and easy to read.

Paper planners are great for weekly and daily tasks. During the Weekly Focus session (Chapter 6), you review projects on the digital task manager and write down the tasks and other details on the paper planner for the week ahead. The following week, you can update the projects and repeat the process.

This is just one example of how they can work together. The key to success is to practice and see what systems and routines work best for you. After some practice, you will know the purpose of each tool and where it fits into the whole planning system.

Introducing the Workbox

The *workbox* may be a new term for you; it's something that Pete started to say on the podcast when he was describing the tools he uses to manage his time and tasks. It makes sense; this is where he finds his work, and most importantly, it doesn't include just one tool. It's a combination of tools that work together to keep his projects organized.

Two Mandatory Components

The workbox is part of your complete planning system. The tools in your workbox do not work alone. They each have a job in your planning system and depend on each other to give you the information you need at the right time. You will learn more about these connections when you learn about workflows in Part 3.

The workbox cannot function without a calendar and task manager (see Figure 5.2).

If you don't want to add any other tools but these two, your workbox can function, but without these two tools, your planning system will fail.

- The calendar keeps track of what, when, and where you need to be.
- The task manager tracks projects and tasks.

Other Planning Tools

Until now, you may not have realized how many tools you use daily that assist your workbox. Partly this is because we are not taught how to use these tools together; we are taught how to use them independently. This is why you end up with having random pieces of paper with tasks

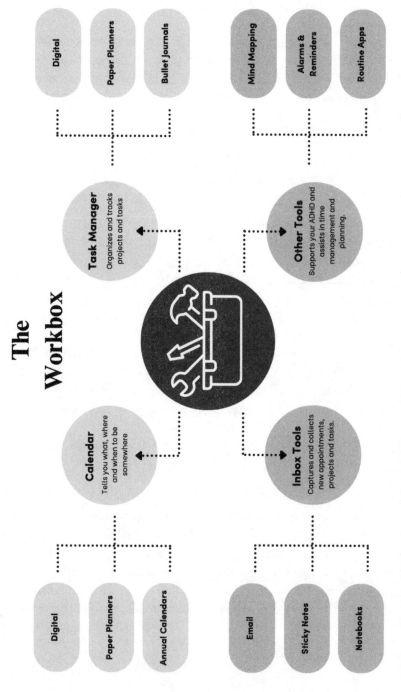

The Workbox

Task Manager
Organizes and tracks projects and tasks
- Digital
- Paper Planners
- Bullet Journals

Other Tools
Supports your ADHD and assists in time management and planning.
- Mind Mapping
- Alarms & Reminders
- Routine Apps

Calendar
Tells you what, where and when to be somewhere
- Digital
- Paper Planners
- Annual Calendars

Inbox Tools
Captures and collects new appointments, projects and tasks.
- Email
- Sticky Notes
- Notebooks

Figure 5.2   The Calendar + Task Manager = Workbox.

to do and appointments that were set and need to somehow get into your calendar.

Maybe the task from the sticky note gets to the task manager, or maybe not. I'm going to guess more often it doesn't find the task manager because there hasn't been a plan, routine, or process to transfer it. This won't be the case for you for too much longer, as you will soon learn that transfer is also a part of having a complete planning system.

Here are a few examples of how other tools support your systems:

- **Daily checklists:** One page with your schedule and priorities for the day
- **Notebooks:** Great for taking notes and writing down information
- **Whiteboards:** For task lists, important dates, reminders, and grocery lists
- **Bulletin boards:** To hold physical paper like invitations and flyers for special events
- **Binders:** Used for larger projects like wedding planning and home remodeling
- **Clipboards:** Assign each clipboard a purpose to its designated list or project
- **Notecards:** Quick, easy way to write your daily task list
- **Sticky notes:** Quick, easy way to write a new task or information that comes in
- **Planner supplies:** Pens, highlighters, stickers, ribbons, and so on
- **Routine apps:** To track daily and weekly routines
- **Alarms:** For reminders and to keep you on task

When these planning tools are built into your planning workflow, they support your ADHD. You don't have to deny yourself the low effort it takes to grab a sticky note to write a new task because you have a complete planning system you trust. The sticky note has a job to do in conjunction with other tools. During your planning sessions, those tasks will be transferred to the workbox's two key tools: the calendar and/or task manager.

Planning Tip

Considering the relationship between ADHD and time, it's best not to assume you know what time it is or expect to remember when your next doctor's appointment is scheduled. The last tool mentioned on the list above is alarms, but it's not limited only to the notifications you get from the workbox. Consider a kitchen timer, a stopwatch, or whatever beeps and grabs your attention. To avoid ignoring reminders, ensure each one serves a distinct purpose and is set at the right time. What if your alarms were only set to remind you to transition to another activity or to get ready to leave for an appointment? These serve different purposes and are more likely to be useful. Alarms don't work if you ignore them, so consider rotating alarm sounds to grab your attention; novelty is good for the ADHD mind. If you constantly ignore them, investigate why this is the case and modify your approach.

Mind Mapping

Mind mapping is an excellent tool for seeing how things are connected visually (Wikipedia). It's a diagram that organizes information into a hierarchy showing relationships among pieces of the whole. It is often created around a single concept, drawn as an image in the center of a blank page, to which associated representations of ideas such as images, words, and parts of words are added. You can do this with blank paper, drawing a circle for the brain, or downloading a mind-mapping app. Figure 5.3 shows an example of a mind map for a bedtime routine.

Mind mapping is a useful tool for several reasons:

- It allows you to write as you think and visualize how it's all connected. It's more natural and intuitive to the way ADHD processes information.
- It's a great way to break projects down before you enter them into your system. It's a rough draft of the outline you'll eventually build into your systems.

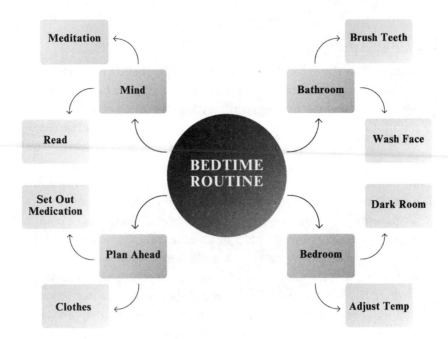

Figure 5.3   Mind map example.

- Using a mind map for brainstorming is a fun and creative way to develop new ideas.
- It's a good place to start if you feel overwhelmed, mapping out your thoughts, and the flexibility means you can change whatever you want.

Overall, mind mapping provides a visual, flexible, and engaging approach to organizing information and ideas, making it a valuable tool for individuals with ADHD. It improves focus, memory, organization, and creativity while accommodating the nonlinear thinking style commonly associated with ADHD.

It's great to have a variety of tools in your workbox. The ADHD mind loves variety, but it doesn't love chaos. Chaos comes when the tools have too many jobs, and you can't find what you need when you need it because you're not sure where you put it. Now it's time to learn more about how to put this system together.

Introducing the Workflow

I mentioned earlier that the other planning tools you choose cannot stand alone. When I say they are a part of a complete planning system, I mean they all serve a specific purpose. The purpose is to keep your projects and tasks organized and tell you where to be, when to be there, and what to do.

You cannot rely on your memory when you have ADHD.

Systems break when the tools are seen as independent from each other (see Figure 5.4).

For example, the purpose of your calendar is to hold your appointments. Let's say you're on the phone with your boss, and they tell you the date of the next team meeting. You don't have time to open your digital calendar, so you grab a sticky note and write the date and time.

During the same call they delegate to you the outline of the agenda, which needs to be sent out to the team the day before the meeting. The boss starts to explain what will be on the agenda but the sticky

Figure 5.4 **All your tools work together in your workflow.**

note is too small for this information, so you grab a notebook and start taking notes. The call ends just in time for your next meeting. You don't do anything with this new information; the sticky note is on the paper from the notebook.

Many things can happen in this scenario. Instead of telling you everything that could go wrong, I want to show you what can go right because you have invested in a planning system for yourself.

Later, you return to your desk. You notice the sticky note and paper. First, you enter the meeting time into your calendar because this is where appointments go. You set a reminder for the meeting. You throw away the sticky note.

Next, you look at the notebook. This notebook is part of your complete planning system. During the call, the information about the agenda could not fit on a tiny sticky note, so you grabbed the notebook. This notebook's job is to collect notes exactly like this one. You review the notes and identify the tasks, such as outlining the agenda and sending it to the team. You add the tasks to your task management system. Your next steps depend on what kind of task manager you use. Include any essential details, like due dates, priority, and so on.

Notes from the discussion about the agenda need to go somewhere. If you use a digital system, include the notes with the task and discard the paper. If you use a paper planner, keep the notebook until you finish the task.

Let's review how these tools work together:

- The sticky note is a convenient, easy way to document information.
- The notebook is assigned for notes. Even if you don't get to it until later, you know where the information is if you need it.
- Part of the workflow is having a routine to enter the information from the sticky note and notebook into your essential planning tools, the calendar, and the task manager.
- If the transfer does not happen on the day, you will be reminded again during the Weekly Focus and Daily Detour sessions (Chapter 10).

If these tools didn't have specific jobs and had no connection to each other whatsoever, can you see how easily chaos and overwhelm could build up in your day?

Here is an exercise to map out the planning system to assist you in organizing your workbox and remembering what is most important as you search for the right tools. The intention is to have a rough draft of your workflow so you can see how each tool works when a new project, task, or appointment comes in:

- Review your "Personal Data Summary" worksheet (Worksheet 3) and write down the must-haves and nice-to-haves on the "Workbox Requirements" worksheet (**Worksheet 8** in the appendix).
- Using the "Your Custom Workbox" worksheet (**Worksheet 9** in the appendix), list each tool, and define its purpose and how it connects with the whole system.

Figure 5.5 shows an example of the "Workbox Requirements" worksheet, and Figure 5.6 shows an example of the "Your Custom Workbox" worksheet.

Example:

Complete the table below of *Must-Haves* and *Nice-to-Haves* for your planning tools. Then, you can use this as your cheat sheet when researching new tools for your workbox.

Planning Tools	Must-Haves	Nice-to-Haves
Calendar	Digital, Reminders, Color Code, Sharing Options	AI features
Task Manager	Easy file structure to keep track of projects and break them into tasks	Different views of the list, Calendar
Paper Planner	Monthly and Weekly View	Long-term planning, Habit tracking

Figure 5.5 Sample "Workbox Requirements" worksheet.

Your Custom Workbox

This is an outline of your workbox. It includes each tool, the purpose of the tool, and how it connects to the workbox.

Planning Tools	Purpose	Connection
Calendar	For appointments, meetings, and intentional planning	Tells me where to be and when; day and time. Set reminders. Update daily and during weekly focus.
Annual Whiteboard Calendar	In office. To see the year at once. Only major events on here.	Visual layout of time to see future due dates and special events. Update monthly.
Todoist	Holds projects and tasks. Breaks them down to see where I'm at with each project.	Main project planner. Update daily and during the weekly focus.
Daily Checklist	Fill out just for the day. Keeps me focused on top priorities of the day. Could be used to capture misc. tasks.	Use when needed. If I have any new tasks, they need to be entered into Todoist. Recycle when done.
One notebook	Stays on desk for quick entry of ideas, tasks, and whatever I don't want to forget.	Transfer information to workbox when needed. Notes will go into note system. Cross off once entered, to remind me I did something with the information.

Figure 5.6   Sample "Your Custom Workbox" worksheet.

Avoid Cluttering Your Workbox

If some notes are discarded after you enter them into the system, what happens to the notes and resources you want to keep around? Say you're planning a trip, and you want to keep all the reference material in one place. Where do you keep a list of books you want to read, movies to watch, or even information from a newsletter that you want to read someday? Sure, a digital task manager could hold this information, but it can also clutter a system with unrelated noise. Noise is a distraction.

We face the same choices around our reference systems that we face in the other areas of our workbox. Are you working mostly digitally? Do you print everything for filing in a drawer or a three-ring binder? The choice is yours, as always. Whatever choice you make, opt for simplicity.

To prevent losing trust in your workbox, it's helpful to think of it as a place that holds only projects and tasks.

There are always exceptions, but reference material is generally stored in a different system. I prefer keeping them separate because it prevents work on current projects and tasks from getting lost. Plus, these notes and reference material can make people feel bad because they never get back to reviewing what they've saved.

A client of mine was saving newsletters and blog posts in her workbox under the category "To Read." The folder was getting larger every day, and it was a constant reminder of what she didn't have time for but felt like she *should* be doing. Yikes! This was not supporting her ADHD.

I recommend adopting a system that works like a digital filing cabinet to store resource material and notes.

While all the reasons we celebrate digital systems hold true, the biggest reason I recommend digital filing cabinets can be summed up in one word: *Search.* Let computers do what they are great at doing. Most modern systems are built on top of software you don't have to understand at all as long as you can find the search box. Some of my clients use their computer's file system—the Finder on macOS or File Explorer on Windows—and build their file system in folders without investing in more complicated software packages at all.

To make a digital filing system work, we need to discuss file *types*. The type of a file defines what applications can read that file. For example, a *.docx* file can be opened by Microsoft Word or any application that opens Word files. A *.pdf* file can be opened by Adobe Acrobat Reader or any application that can open PDF files.

File types get old. If you've ever tried to open a document you wrote on your first computer back in high school or college or in your first job and learned sadly that the file type is not recognized, you learned the hard way how developers sometimes just stop supporting their applications and file types. Documents created using those applications are lost to history.

Two file types have emerged as winners of the file system archive game. The first is simply Plain Text, or files ending in .txt. The first computers outputted plain text, and the format is still a cornerstone of modern development. Save an important email in plain text and you'll have it for years to come.

The problem with plain text is that it does not support images, layout, or even color. Over the years, PDF has emerged as a terrific archive file format for file systems because it's universal—it can be opened on a wide variety of computer systems—and it's open source, meaning many different developers and organizations have a shared vested interest in continuing to support it. Even better, many applications offer a simple *File —> Save As. . .* (or *Export As. . .*) *PDF* command, allowing you to take an existing document of any file type on your computer, save it as a PDF to your file system, and be confident that you'll have it as reference material for as long as you'll need it. You can find more information on digital preservation along with a more detailed list of formats you can trust in your own file system from the Digital Preservation Coalition (www.dpconline.org).

If you want to make sure you review the resources from time to time, don't rely on your memory. Instead, add a recurring task to pop up at the end of every week or month. At whatever frequency you feel comfortable reviewing new information in your system is exactly how often you will want to remind yourself to check those file folders.

If you don't have time, don't worry about it. The information is there when you need it, but it's no longer cluttering your task manager. Remember, there's no *should* here. Who cares if you never return to the information? In my opinion, not reading a blog post or newsletter you archived is not worth the effect that shame has on our self-esteem.

Now is the time to focus on the planning system tools and let go of the idea that everything must fit into one tool. You can look at note systems later.

Take Planning to the Next Step

I don't think this will surprise many of you, but just in case you didn't know, the ADHD mind has a hard time making decisions. It's true. I've seen people struggle with all kinds of decisions, from choosing wrapping paper to moving to a new city. Something else happens when it has to do with any kind of product: research can take hours, and the more you research, the more unsure you are about what to do. This leads to paralysis and no decision is made. And no decision means no progress on moving forward.

You've heard of FOMO (Fear of Missing Out), right? It's pretty much the driving force behind social media behavior. But did you know that the term's originator, Patrick McGinnis, came up with a cousin acronym that hits home much better for ADHDers?

It's FOBO, or Fear of Better Options, and it describes precisely what we must address when making decisions.

Choosing the wrong one is the fear, but what if you choose the right one? Most digital and paper systems are very similar to each other. If you find a system that supports your ADHD and you like it, don't fear FOBO. Make the decision and focus on learning the system. Practicing using the system is the only way you will know if something works. If you find it's not what you thought it would be, changing your mind is OK.

To prevent the rabbit hole of research, set a deadline to decide.

I suggest one week—yes, I said one week. This is the window of time that I give my clients, and I'm giving the same to you. It requires you to challenge your FOBO, limiting beliefs, and perfectionism. The sooner you decide, the sooner the transformation of how you relate to the world begins.

When choosing a digital system, keep in mind that free versions only give a small sample of what the system can do. Once you find one that works, pay for the upgrade to get the maximum potential. This doesn't mean you must use all 100-plus features, but at least you can access them. It's a small investment that greatly impacts your daily life.

With Great Power Comes Great Responsibility

Spider-Man is my *jam*, and as much as I'd love to continue this essay on a path of extraordinary nerdery, I'm not going to do that. I'm not going to tell you that your planning tools should not require the articulated cybernetic tentacles of Doc Ock to manage. I certainly won't mention that too many planning tools could take over your life like the alien symbiote did to the unsuspecting Eddie Brock. And under *no circumstances* will I even *mention* that the advanced planning technology we have at our collective fingertips today could make us feel as powerful—and delusional—as Norman Osborne!

The title of this essay is ripped from the pages of *Amazing Fantasy #15*, the first-ever comic appearance of Peter Parker as Spider-Man in 1962. In the story, Peter had just appeared on TV, and on his way out of the studio he let a burglar escape. The guy just ran right on by. When a police officer asked why Spidey hadn't tried to trip the guy, the wallcrawler said, "Sorry, pal, that's *your* job!" Long story short, Peter wasn't a good guy, and that same burglar ended up shooting Peter's uncle because karma. And as Peter walks into the night, learning his lesson, the narrator marks the final panel with ". . . at last in this world, with great power there must also come—great responsibility."

OK, I just did a nerd thing and went on far too long about the first appearance of Spider-Man when I swore to you I wouldn't. Did I mention I have ADHD? Thanks for hanging out with me. It's good to have friends. Now let me try to bring this horse into the barn.

I'm a guy who has spent a lot of time with planning tools. I was a Day Runner guy. I moved from there to Franklin Quest. Then the Covey Leadership Center bought Franklin Quest in 1997 and became Franklin Covey. That didn't make any sense to me, so I moved from paper to digital.

Data entry took about a week of cereal-only dining into Lotus Organizer, a perfectly skeuomorphic day planner complete with pages that turned into a ringed binder on screen. That only lasted as long as it took me to save up for an Apple Newton MessagePad 2100 in 1997. Apple canceled that in 1998, so I moved to Palm.

I'm going to stop with the history lesson here because it's not even the year 2000 yet and let me tell you things get *crazy* in 2007.

The story here isn't about the litany of tools. What I shudder to think about is the process. When I was still using the paper planner, every leap cost days of rewriting contacts and schedules and assignments and plans. When I moved to the hybrid system, every week, I would sit at my printer and print out updated contact pages, punch holes in them, and meticulously enter them in my binders.

Digital systems brought their own costs. It's only recently that we've been able to capture some degree of interoperability in calendars and contacts. Take solace in the syncing and merging tools we have at our disposal because for those of us who remember the *before times*, we know that the costs of integrating brought only disarray and confusion into our lives in the form of unfinished migrations, missed meetings, and dropped contacts. With all that in mind, here are some thoughts that Compromised Pete often wishes he had thought through before he embarked on yet another system migration.

There are no two ways about it: we have an overabundance of options in our selection of planning tools.

My ADHD brain has trouble doing simple scenario planning without using the tools so I end up in the position of signing up for a *lot* of trials and entering my own data to see how the tools perform not just under load, but under *my* load. It sounds like a lot of work, I know, but this is effectively my needs analysis. By loading the tool with my own work, I get a sense of what should be in the tool, what should go somewhere else, and what should be dropped completely.

The choice usually comes down to one of customization versus complexity: what is the trade-off between a highly

(*continued*)

(*continued*)

customizable tool that allows me to accomplish incredibly complex tasks when measured against simple tools that are fast but feature-light?

When I wrote, "It sounds like a lot of work, I know," that was a bit of narrative sleight of hand. I didn't want you to think too hard about it because the reality is that it is an extraordinary amount of work, and the cognitive load that comes with focusing on managing multiple tools while hyper-focusing on a new app-testing cycle can be disastrous. When evaluating a new work management/task system, for example, I simultaneously tested four tools by importing all my work into each of them and using them side by side for a month. Add a task? Add it four times, Jordan. Finish a task? You guessed it: check it off four times. I'm a huge believer in performing a regular review of the tools we use, but I don't recommend doing it my way. This is the ADHD dance. I know better than to ask so much of myself, and I know that the allure of new tools is the light, and I am the sad, predictable moth.

What do I get out of a regular review? This is the best part of any good system review: I get to see where I've introduced friction in my work.

What Is Friction?

Friction is any part of a workflow that can allow ADHD distraction to sneak in and reduce the likelihood of effective task completion.

Here's a quick list of the kinds of systemic friction I'm looking for both in my own work and in the work I do on larger projects with others:

- **Physical friction:** Is the hardware I'm using outdated or slow? Is my workspace cluttered to the point that I can't find what I need when I need it?
- **Digital friction:** Are the apps and digital tools I'm using unintuitive? Do the tools communicate with one another

easily or do they require excessive manual transfer of information?

- **Cognitive friction:** Am I needlessly switching between tasks without completion? Do I have too many choices to make in how to complete a task that I run into decision paralysis?
- **Emotional friction:** Does the process elevate stress and anxiety? Am I working on tasks that don't align with my own values?
- **Process friction:** Does the process include too many steps or approvals that slow it down? Are the goals for the task clear before work has begun?
- **Communication friction:** Do I have all the information I need to begin work? Does information flow freely between systems and stakeholders?
- **Temporal friction:** Are meetings and deadlines in concert with my own peak zones of productivity? Have we included time zone planning in task coordination?

Ask yourself, Jordan, how often have you found yourself frustrated because of friction of the sort we're talking about here? If you have, then you have some work to do.

- Streamline your processes and remove any and all steps that aren't required to get the work done successfully.
- Optimize your tools to fit the work; if your computer is too slow but you spend your day editing and rendering video, get a new computer.
- Reorient your environment to minimize distractions and maximize ease of use . . . and buy a plant.
- Centralize communication channels for clear information sharing.
- Get trained up! Make sure the tools you count on every day are tools you've invested the time in to become a functional expert in their use.

(continued)

(*continued*)

We have incredible choice and power in the tools we can use to organize our work and our lives. We're on the cusp of new tools that effectively "think" for us, organize our work, and keep us on track with barely any intervention from our meaty mitts at all.

Along the way, we have to remember the core tenets of our own brand of ADHD. For me, if I don't have a system that is fun to use, easy to master, and intuitive, I know I'll be distracted and ineffective.

Wait, Jordan . . . do you hear that? Do you hear the dramatic music swelling behind us as I write this? Do you see me standing proudly, high on a rooftop, a silhouette against the setting sun behind me? Cue the heroic ending!

This is the essence, the pulsing heart of my Spidey-centric philosophy. Every byte of creation, every pixel of organization, every whisper of automation that courses through the veins of my digital existence comes with a weighty responsibility—a pact to wield these tools with intention and care. They are extensions of our will, our values, and our most deeply held ambitions, and we must embrace them with a reverence that honors that truth. Out there, in the web of our interconnected lives, are souls who place their trust in us, who lean on the frameworks we build, and who depend on the constellations we chart in the chaos. It is our solemn duty to don the mantle, to equip ourselves with the finest of these digital armors so that when the moment calls, we stand ready—unwavering, unyielding—to uphold the promise not to falter, not to fail.

This is my credo, my unwavering commitment as I navigate this labyrinth of ones and zeroes: I shall honor their trust, rise to the occasion, and be the hero they deserve, cloaked in the digital might of our age, yet ever mindful of the human heart that beats in our core.

Coach's Corner

You may question why I recommend only spending a week choosing your tools. I've seen people stay indecisive for too long, and it only worsens their chaos. If it's taking longer to decide, ask more questions to figure out what's blocking you.

Here are a few to think about:

- What are your top two choices?
- What are the pros and cons of each?
- What's holding you back from deciding?
- What's your best-case scenario?
- What's the worst-case scenario?
- What else do you need to decide?

Talk through your answers with someone else; this helps organize your thoughts, and another opinion might help you reach a decision. Lastly, decide and get started. You've got this.

Chapter Summary

The following are the key points from the chapter:

- Set a deadline to decide.
- Decide what tools to include in your system.
- Make a list of each tool and its function.
- For digital systems, sign up for free trials.
- Visit the office supplies store to look at paper planners.
- Review websites and watch videos on different tools.
- Zero in on your top two choices.
- Decide and move on to the next chapter!

Congratulations on deciding the best tools to support you! This is no easy task, and you did it. In the next chapter, you will build your workbox to organize projects and tasks in a way that makes sense to you, supports your ADHD, and will be resilient when plans go a bit sideways. And just so you know, plans fall sideways, backward, forwards, and in all kinds of directions. Soon, you will have the confidence to be just as flexible.

6

Step 2: Building the Workbox

WE KNOW THE best tools in the toolbox do not make us carpenters. We first learn how to use the tools and practice to improve each time we build something new. The same is true for your workbox. You spent the time researching and deciding on the right tools for you.

Now it's time for step 2, which is about building the workbox. This means learning how to use your planning tools. We don't become experts at anything overnight—it takes time and practice. A calendar or new planner will only work if you know how to use it and set it up to do the jobs you need it to do.

Let's get started!

Getting off the Hamster Wheel

My family was blessed to have two hamsters, Wilbur and Link, and they loved their wheels; they were fast, going nowhere. This was entertaining for them, but when you're on the hamster wheel of failed planners, it's anything but fun.

Unfortunately, many planning tools fail before they are given a chance to succeed, and it's because step 2 of building out the tools was incomplete or not set up to be resilient to being ignored or forgotten about. The most common scenario is that the tool is bought and has your attention for a few weeks. Then, suddenly, the tool no longer has your attention. You just took your first step onto the hamster wheel.

It is critical to learn how the tools work to prevent this from happening. The only way to learn is to practice and set time aside to do the necessary work. You will learn much more about intentional planning in Chapter 10, but this is an excellent example of where planning is necessary to have a functional and resilient complete planning system.

Schedule Planning Sessions

The most reliable way to ensure you learn and set up your workbox is to schedule it on your calendar like an appointment. Some may think this sounds like a great idea but doubt they will do it. I'm challenging this limiting belief because I want you to consider reframing how you think about this appointment.

Let's approach it in an ADHD-friendly way. Here are a few ways to take the time to build your workbox:

1. Schedule a daily time block for 15 minutes. Schedule it before you start your day, after a break, or at the end of the day. It's only 15 minutes; everything else can wait.
2. Write down where you left off. This makes the transition easier when you come back.
3. If you want to work longer sessions, schedule when you feel your best and do something fun before the session to increase your dopamine.
4. Set a timer and make a game out of it; how many projects can you enter before the time is up? Find ways to make the time more engaging.

For those of you starting from scratch and not transferring data from another tool, this will be a pretty clean process. You will continue to build the system as you use it.

For those transferring data from somewhere else, it can get a bit messier. Some systems allow you to upload the information, but the issue with this option is that if your current system is not up to date, then you are transferring outdated information. It becomes a decision on what is less time-consuming: updating outdated data or creating new data by referencing the old data. There is also the option of archive. This means you keep the data tucked away so it doesn't clutter the updated tool.

The longer you are in between systems, the more likely both tools break because you don't trust them.

Keep track of what you've entered and what's left so transitions are easier for the scheduled time block and other open times during the day.

Planning Tip

Words matter, and what you see on your calendar will inspire or make you run away. Seeing a time block for "planning" will probably not inspire you; take a moment to think about what will.

Here are a few ideas:

- Creating Time
- Crafting My Best Life
- Designing Balance
- Freedom

Time Is of the Essence

Some of you will understand the value of setting up the system quickly, and some may think, *I'll get to it when I can*. This is not as urgent as doing the work on the lists. I get it, and I hear this all the time. But guess what happens? Later doesn't come. Without your attention *and* intention, this becomes one more system that did not work.

The investment of time you put into building your workbox will pay off immensely sooner than you think.

Think about how much time you spend daily feeling stressed about what you may have forgotten, guilty of missing a meeting, anxious about a presentation because you were unprepared, disappointed that you didn't start sooner, mad because tasks take longer than you think.

Now, imagine a world where you trust your workbox. It's not perfect, but it's better than anything you've ever had. You are more confident and realistic about your time.

Your system is resilient, so even if it's been neglected for a few days, you can return to it, update it, and get back to using it.

You may still be afraid of what you'll find, but you are no longer on the hamster wheel. You have a complete planning system, and you got it by taking the time to set it up.

System Fragility

Finance. Energy. Transportation. Shipping and supply chain. Telecom. Government and defense. If you're reading this and you're in one of those sectors professionally, allow me to apologize right up front. This brief aside covers system fragility, and I know that your understanding of the concept is going to be comically more advanced than my description here. I beg your patience as I bring a very big thing down to a more modest scale.

You see, Jordan, in some industries, system fragility is a representation of risks that exist in highly optimized and complex systems. Think of it like this: when you order a new Blitzwow G9 laptop online, it likely comes from a factory in Shenzhen, China, which is situated on the mainland, just north of Hong Kong. From the manufacturer, that laptop will be boxed up and moved around the world by plane or—if the manufacturer is transitioning to the more environmentally palatable—ship before it lands in our fair country. At our border it will meet with customs agents, who will inspect and eventually allow the product to enter the country. Then, by truck or plane and a collection of carrier partners, the Blitzwow will wind its way to your door.

That simplification already includes a number of points at which, if something breaks down, the system breaks down entirely. This sort of supply chain system is an incredibly complicated web of interconnected pieces that together can appear to be magical. But when one domino falls, the whole system is at risk.

Now, I'm not a logistics expert, so let us proceed at ADHD scale. When you consider your own suite of productivity tools, how would you rate their level of strength?

I use a suite of tools to hold my life together. One of my workbox apps is called TickTick, and it serves as home to everything I have to do. My calendar is an app called Fantastical, and once I have things to do that deserve time to do them, they are reflected in Fantastical. My company uses the email app Spark Mail, and that is my primary inbox, though we also use Discord for team communication extensively. Those apps mark the core of my communication and work management system. They communicate with one another such that I can share tasks and events back and forth, send emails to either TickTick or Fantastical, and thus know what I'm doing any given day and when I am to do it.

Beyond that core system, I use apps for production. I produce all my podcasts using Logic Pro and record the audio using Audio Hijack from Rogue Amoeba Software. I use a combination of design applications from Adobe and Affinity Software. I write in Obsidian and Ulysses. The list goes on and on.

Those apps mark my extended system. They connect with my primary productivity system manually in that when I finish performing a task—producing a podcast in Logic, for example—I move over to TickTick and check the box, marking it complete. In that way, I am a central part of my productivity system, too.

There are a few other benefits in my system that come naturally as a part of the choices I make of platform and app, too. They are all digital tools and part of a syncing ecosystem. If I'm strolling along a woodland bridge with my dog and he lunges at a wily raccoon, knocking my phone out of my hand and into the rushing rapids below, I am safe. My data is backed up and synced between multiple devices. That redundancy makes the system resilient.

"But Pete," you're saying, "I hate computers and stuff. I just want to write things down and use my paper system. It's foolproof!"

It is, Jordan. You're right.

But also . . . is it?

The Perils of Paper Systems

As I have referenced elsewhere, I was once a Franklin Quest planner guy. I wrote in it every day, journaling briefly, scheduling often, and updating contact lists indefinitely. I loved the system,

(continued)

(*continued*)

the page design, and the feel of the leather binder; I carried it with me everywhere.

If I got distracted one day and didn't look at my written reminders, I would simply *miss* them. There was no beeping or booping of an alert to tell me that something was about to happen. There was no system to move missed tasks to the current day automatically. They were simply skipped. I would move through bouts of hyper-focus on my planner, spending hours writing information about myself and my schedule, and then I might put it down for days. As such, my part of my own system was too large. I was introducing fragility because I couldn't be reliably counted on to maintain my own system.

Do we need to review what happens when the wily raccoon meets the herky-jerky dog and the *paper* planner falls into the comically hyperbolic rushing rapids?

In order to refine my own system work and productivity system, I had to start thinking about each and every intersection where tools and processes meet. There are a few areas where those interactions can become true trouble spots.

Interrogating the Systems

First question: How reliant am I on any specific platform, manufacturer, or developer? As a Franklin user, I was furiously devoted to the design of their pages. They worked exactly as my mind worked. When the Covey organization bought them out and began introducing tools and pages in greater alignment with their *Seven Habits* methodology, I realized just how fragile my own system turned out to be.

The answer to this first question is to consider how important the tool's design is to my workflow and how important it is for me to be able to exert control over it. On one end of the scale would be something like Franklin Covey with their templated pages and blanks for filling. On the other, consider the Bullet Journal®, a system originated by Ryder Carroll that offers structure and guidance through principle, but relies on you, the user, to design every page by hand. It is your system, bound only by your choice of pen and paper by which you create it.

Second question: How high are the switching costs? Moving from my first paper planner system required many hours of manual data entry. Once done, though, moving from system to system cost me fewer hours as data entry was replaced by copy and paste and eventually eliminated altogether with import and export. Today, my choice of productivity tools is predicated on whether those tools import and export in formats easily accessible by other tools. This reduces those switching costs and allows me to build the suite of productivity tools that suits my brain best, knowing full well that it will have to change over time. My ADHD simply *loves* to change tools.

To review: stick to tools that aren't solely reliant on one manufacturer or developer to continue without change, and choose tools that allow me to reduce switching costs. Got it. Super easy. No problem. Except . . .

"Pete, OK fine. But I work at ExoCarp International and all the tools that I use are handed down to me from our corporate IT department."

I was afraid you'd bring that up.

Because the answer isn't pretty. And it doesn't *feel* good.

A shout-out to my homies in Information Technology and Systems Administration, y'all. They do largely thankless work to ensure that our systems are clean and running smoothly, and much of their job is constrained by contracts and agreements enjoined beyond their pay grade. Working with technology support staff is frustrating because theirs is mostly a job of "can'ts" and "don'ts." And as frustrated as you are, trying to do a job that you know you'd be able to do better if you just had *this one tool*, they are equally frustrated at having to say no, not now, not yet, and "once I get this approved" all the time.

(continued)

(*continued*)

You have choices:

- **Adapt.** Do whatever it takes to build your own expertise in the tools that you are given and use them to your very best ability. I often hear folks argue that this tool or that just doesn't work for them in their jobs without having taken the time to learn. It's possible the tool will work for you, but in a different way than you expect if you just give it a try.
- **Make your case.** Talk to your manager and system administrators and lobby for support to get the accommodation you need for the tools you want. There is a non-zero chance you'll get exactly what you want as soon as you educate your team on the value of the tool for the job.
- **You could always dual-wield.** That's right, you read that. Carry your work phone and your work laptop, and have a different system for your personal life. I recommend this option least of all, and you might be able to guess why. You only have one life, one set of 24 hours in a day. Managing multiple productivity devices or tools requires additional diligence that comes at a cognitive premium.

The fragility inherent in any system ultimately comes down to its flexibility, or lack thereof. When we design productivity systems that are overly rigid or constrained to specific tools, we introduce the risk of system decay or failure. Like a tall oak tree that splinters and cracks in high winds, an inflexible system will shatter at the slightest disruption.

The key is to cultivate resilience through diversity—have backup options for when tools change or break, minimize reliance on any one manufacturer or platform, and reduce switching costs wherever possible. With thoughtfully designed flexibility, our productivity systems can weather any storm. Will mistakes still happen? Of course—no one is perfect. A flexible system forgives the missed reminder or lost planner. It bends so that it need not break.

Buckle Up, Let's Hit the Road

Are you ready to take back control of your time? Imagine, feeling at peace at the end of the day. Now is a great time to review your mission statement from your "Personal Data Summary" worksheet (Worksheet 3). Remember your why for being here.

To get you started on a positive note, below are clear directions on where to start to build your workbox and the actions that follow to complete it to the point of being *good enough* to start using it as soon as possible.

These are the steps to get started:

1. **Schedule time blocks to work on setting up the system.** Set reminders and treat them like any other appointment. Don't let them compete with other appointments; this is a protected time to work only on this. It's temporary but it is a priority.
2. **If you are learning a new system, watch the tutorials and other videos of users demonstrating the tool.** This goes for all tools, not just the digital ones. There is so much value in *seeing* the tool in action. Take notes as you learn about features that work to support your ADHD.
3. **To avoid frustration, set up easy projects and tasks first.** The more detailed and complicated projects can wait. It lets you practice testing the system's features, and you can immediately feel the benefit of a trusted workbox.
4. **Start using the workbox once the project is entered.** The mission is to start using the workbox immediately. When a project has been added, including tasks, begin referencing the workbox each time you work on it. You do not have to wait for *all* projects to be entered. It gives you practice using the tool and you can adjust along the way.

What Time Do We Need to Be There?

Out of the two essential systems, the calendar will be the easiest to update. Include any important dates like birthdays, anniversaries, and upcoming special events. Review what is currently on the calendar and update anything canceled or postponed. Add new meetings, appointments, deadlines, and any other relevant information.

Think about how you want to use your calendar within the rest of the planning system. For example, learn more about the special features, setting recurring events, sharing capabilities, and filtering certain appointments. Rethink how you use alarms and reminders (Chapter 3). If they are getting ignored, it's time to reframe your approach and make them mean something.

Planning Tip

For students, I recommend using a combination of digital and paper planning tools. At the beginning of a new semester, update your class and work schedules, and make them a recurring event. I recommend using digital calendars for appointments because of the built-in reminders. Because with ADHD, out of sight is out of mind, have a whiteboard and wall calendar as part of your workbox. The wall calendar gives you a glance of what's coming up in the future and the whiteboard can be used for reminders of what's happening this week.

Color Coding for ADHD

Color coding is not a new concept, and for the ADHD mind, it's helpful in many ways. Assigning different colors to different types of information or categories helps identify and retrieve relevant information (ADDRC, 2023).

However, with too many colors, the purpose is lost, and it means nothing. This can happen when too many things are scheduled on the calendar—for example, if you share calendars with your family and everybody's calendar shows up at once. This is where the filter option is helpful; it allows you to choose which calendars to view.

When a color is associated with a project or activity, your brain remembers it, and it's easier to find what you are looking for. For example, green (the color of money) is for Work, and yellow (school bus) is for School.

How to Use More Than One Calendar

A common scenario with clients is having one calendar for work and one for home. This isn't necessarily by choice because their jobs require a specific network, and they don't want their personal information on the work calendar.

Because of this, a part of *your* workflow (Chapter 4) requires updating both calendars to ensure nothing gets missed or double booked. This is where reminders on digital calendars are so helpful because you don't want to forget the doctor's appointment scheduled during your workday, and you want to make sure you are unavailable on the work calendar to avoid overbooking.

Now it's time to tackle the task manager!

What Are We Doing When We Get There?

There are so many options for task managers; your approach to setting them up will vary depending on whether you're using digital, paper, or a combination of both. We separated the two kinds of task managers to give you an idea of where to start.

Paper Planner

Generally, paper planners take less time for the initial setup, most are not customizable, and you're limited to the predetermined layout. Take time to learn about it and decide how it fits into the rest of the system.

Here are a few key factors to think about as you set up your planner:

- **Keep supplies together.** Planners are colorful, fun, and exciting to look at. So if you like colors, pens, stickers, and motivational quotes, you will have a great time setting up a planner. To keep your planner supplies together, collect them into a basket or a fun bag and keep them near where you do your weekly and daily planning.
- **Decide how to use the calendar.** Most planners have calendars, meaning you may have two calendars to manage if you use a digital one. Identify what this means for you. Do you need to fill in the paper calendar the same way as the digital one? You get to choose. You may write down key events or due dates on the planner as a security measure so you don't forget. Think about what best supports your ADHD and how the two calendars work together within your complete system.

- **It's okay to change your mind.** Don't force something to work if it's not working. Planners are easier for the initial setup but not easier for maintenance. They require a lot of writing, which requires time and consistency to keep updated. You may feel disappointed because you want this to work, but it's OK. Be proud of yourself for making this decision and finding something better.
- **Consistency is not everything.** Consistency falls under the category of words where the ADHD brain shuts down. Consistency helps, but it's not everything. As you set up your planner, think about what it will be like to return to it after not using it for a day, a week, a month, or longer. If empty pages bring you shame, rip them out. Focus less on consistency and more on how to recover from inconsistency.

Planning Tip

It's not a matter of *whether* you are inconsistent with your workbox; it's *when* you are inconsistent. It will happen, and when it does, I encourage you to stop believing the workbox doesn't work or that it's your fault. This is where understanding how ADHD impacts you is important to remember. You will have excellent weeks and a few where the workbox disappears.

The key to success isn't consistency. It's having a recovery plan. When you have a complete planning system, your recovery time will be cut in half, if not more. You've already done the work, and you have a clear workflow on how your tools are connected and what you need to do to get them updated.

Schedule a time to catch up, and remember that this time is different. Whatever you find, you will be able to clean up. Rip out the empty pages on the paper planner or start with the past due dates using a digital system. These tools update much sooner than you think, and you can start again.

Digital Task Managers

As you learn about the fabulous features, choose the ones that will best support your ADHD. To prevent overwhelm, keep it simple at the beginning. Just because the system has over 100 features doesn't mean you must learn them all at once. The system should feel intuitive, not confusing.

Here are a few key factors to think about as you set up your task manager:

- **Avoid overthinking:** This happens to the best of us. Overthinking a process feels like you trying to detangle yourself from a cobweb. Keep it simple at the beginning. Complicated systems get abandoned because they become too overwhelming or are never used because you are afraid to use them.
- **Avoid perfectionism:** As you build the system's organizational structure, remember that the system you're creating now *will* be different in one month, six months, and one year from now. It doesn't have to be perfect; you need it to be "complete enough" to use.
- **Practice and adjust:** Until you use your system, you have no idea what works and what doesn't. What sounds like an excellent name for a category now may not make sense to you in three months. A new project comes in, and you decide to try something new and organize it differently.

Organizational Structure

Every task manager has an organizational structure, and each system uses a different language. To keep it simple, I will use the following terms: Areas, Projects, and Tasks (see Figure 6.1).

Each area has a set of projects, and each project has a set of tasks:

- **Areas:** These are the main categories where you have different projects. Areas can be broad, like Home, Work, Personal, and School. For example, projects like Remodels, Gardening, and Organizing would fall under Home. Areas can be specific by the type of work, for example, Podcasts, Clients, and ADHD Books. These fall under Work, but I prefer they have their own area. Areas keep our projects organized so you only look at what you want and not everything at once.

ORGANIZATIONAL STRUCTURE

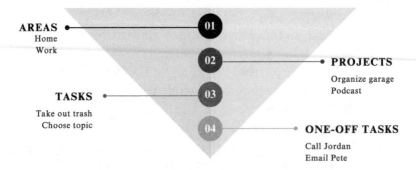

Figure 6.1   Organizational structure.

- **Projects:** Under each area, there are projects related to that area and include more than one task to complete. They are concrete and have a beginning and end. Projects can take an hour to days, weeks, or even months. Digital task managers are structured to break down large projects into tasks and subtasks. For example, under the area of Work, I have projects that include ADHD Book, Website, Travel.
- **Tasks:** These are the specific actions needed to complete projects. However, they can also stand alone. They are smaller actions and more defined. For example, under Website, tasks could include reviewing the website, creating a list of changes, Email updates to Pete, and Review updates. These tasks may have subtasks and due dates; digital systems are set up to help organize the details.

The one-off tasks can be those that do not belong to a project, like Call Carol, Order flowers, Buy gift. They could fall under the area of Personal and create a project name like Birthdays or To Do This Week.

Planning Tip

Attach a verb to the task description to avoid any confusion about what you need to do. For example, email Jordan, call Mom, or file papers. When tasks are too vague, they usually get avoided or must be broken down further. The next time you are unsure what to do, ask what the verb is to break through the avoidance.

Projects versus Tasks

One of the reasons tasks are avoided is because the task is not just one task, it's several tasks. If it takes more than one action to complete, it's most likely a project. Sometimes even a verb is insufficient to figure out what to do next. For example, "Organize Garage" is too vague. The garage is a large space, so what are you organizing? Where do you start? How do you know you're done? If you don't know the answers to the questions, it's easy to think you'll just do this *later*. This is an example of where a task within a project has subtasks.

If there is more than one step within the task, break it down into further steps until you are clear on the first step to take.

Breaking Projects Down

Once you figure out that the task is a project, the most practical strategy is to break the project down into tasks. This strategy is everywhere; I recommend it all the time because it makes sense. However, this is not an intuitive skill for ADHD. The strategy suggests breaking down the project to make it easier to start, but how do you start breaking down the project?

Here's a guide on how to break projects down:

- **Identify the outcome.** Think about the result. How will you know this project is complete? Write down any important details about the project, like important milestones, deadlines, and resources.
- **Brainstorm the action steps.** Write down whatever comes to mind. Don't worry about the order or whether you have listed everything. You can always add to the list later as things come up.

- **Order the tasks.** Figure out which tasks on the master list need to happen first before other tasks can be done. Consider other people who are involved in the project.
- **Prioritize tasks.** As you review the tasks, prioritize the tasks in order of importance.
- **Tasks with subtasks.** As you sort the tasks, you may notice larger tasks that have subtasks. Write these out because you will include them in the workbox later.

This strategy has the potential for perfectionism to sneak into your thought process. This is a warning to be aware of overcomplicating the process. Consider this a rough draft—you don't need to know the milestones or due dates; you can enter them when relevant.

Break Tasks Down as Far as You Need to Get Started   There's a balance between being clear about what the next action is and having too many details that clutter the list, which makes it overwhelming to look at and then it gets ignored. Finding the right balance for you may vary depending on the task.

If Procrastination Is an Issue, Find the Smallest Point of Entry   For example, Unload Dishwasher. It's a clear task; I know what to do, but I don't want to do it.

To get started, I will break it down into tiny tasks.

Unload Dishwasher

- Open dishwasher door.
- Pull out top tray.
- Put away dishes from top tray.
- Pull out bottom tray.
- Put away dishes from bottom tray.
- Put away silverware.
- Close dishwasher door.

Depending on your energy level, these tiny tasks can be done separately or all at once. The point is to find the smallest entry to start the task. Task initiation is one of the executive functions that ADHDers struggle with. Knowing that all I have to do right now is open the dishwasher door gets the task started and lessens the overwhelm of having to do it all at once.

Planning Tip

Breaking projects down into smaller tasks requires making decisions and being able to identify the details. If you find you are struggling with any part of this process, consider walking through the steps with another person. People with ADHD are verbal processors; it helps to talk about your thoughts and how you see the pieces fit together. The other person can ask questions to help you make the decisions you are stuck on.

Entering Areas, Projects, and Tasks into the Workbox

Setting up your workbox requires deciding on your areas and breaking projects down into tasks. Here's a step-by-step process to help you get started.

Grab a piece of paper and pen and follow these directions:

1. Make a list of areas in your life that have projects.
2. Identify the projects under each area.
3. Enter the areas and projects into your system.
4. Choose one project (one that is not complicated).
5. On a piece of paper, write down the details of the project.
6. Brainstorm the tasks required to complete the project. (Think about the end goal and then work backward on the steps to achieve the goal.)
7. Prioritize tasks by level of importance. Think about deadlines and the order in which tasks need to be completed.
8. Enter the project and tasks in the system.
9. When working on this project, open the task manager to mark completed tasks and update project details as needed.
10. Repeat steps 4–9 until all the projects you want in the system are completed.

What Does "Complete" Mean?

It doesn't mean that all your information must be entered to start using it. We want it to be complete enough that when you work on a specific project, you refer to the new tool to tell you what's next. The days of perfection and absolute thinking are long gone. Congratulations—you are well on your way to creating a complete planning system that works for you!

Coach's Corner

The workbox is always a work in progress. You may notice that an area is getting too cluttered with too many projects, and you can't find what you need; this doesn't mean the entire workbox isn't working. It means it's time to rethink the organizational structure of that one area to something that is more consolidated and cleaner.

Setting up a new system carries a mix of emotions: excitement for a new approach but self-doubt that it may not work. If this comes up for you, remember that you are approaching this differently than before, and what if it does work? Challenge those old beliefs and believe that planning with ADHD is possible.

Chapter Summary

The following are the key points from the chapter:

- Set time aside in your schedule to build the system.
- Cultivate resilience through diversity.
- Design flexible systems.
- Learn about your tools.
- Color code where that works best.
- Know the difference between areas, projects, and tasks.
- Set up your workbox by breaking down projects.

Congratulations! I can't wait for you to start using your new workbox. It's a great sense of relief when you know you can find information about the projects you're working on in one place. Now it's time to move on to the next step of creating your planning system: maintaining the workbox.

Let's get started!

7

Step 3: Maintaining the Workbox

WHEN YOUR VEHICLE'S gas tank gets low, you go to a gas station to fill it up. It doesn't mean it's time to buy a new car. To keep it running, you will fill it up with gas every time you need to do it for as long as you want to drive the vehicle.

Think of your workbox like your vehicle. It will start running out of gas when you haven't looked at it for a while. However, this alone doesn't mean it's time to invest in new planning tools. One planning session may be the gas you need to get it back into a working system. If more maintenance needs to be done, it may take a few more sessions.

Just like vehicles can't run without gas, workboxes stop working if you stop paying attention to them. Because this is where you manage your work, they need your attention regularly.

Before I go any further, how do you feel about the word "routine"?

We have long advocated for rethinking the language that defines the ADHD experience. Specific words carry many emotions. A client told me he would rather have a root canal than set goals. Another client shared that hearing me say *planning* made her anxiety level increase to a 10 (on a scale of 1–10). Someone told me the word "structure" made them feel like they were in jail and routines felt restricting.

These triggers are connected to your thoughts, experiences, and memories.

The client who obviously is not a fan of setting goals associates the word with failure; he doesn't need another reminder of everything he's

119

not doing. Many people with ADHD resist structure despite thriving in it, fearing it will take away their free spirit.

In the ADHD productivity space, this becomes incredibly challenging. You're conditioned to think of your tasks as an obligation.

- I *have* to write that report.
- I *should* clean my house today.
- I *need* a routine around planning.

I have yet to meet anyone who wants to plan for tasks they have to do, let alone set up a routine for planning. But what happens in your brain when you reattune yourself from the space of obligation to one of opportunity?

There will always be things on our lists that we have to do; it's a part of life, but there are also many things we *get* to do. Planning opens up opportunities to make time for those things.

In this light, planning and routines shed their baggage of obligation and become instead the helpful structures we put in place to help take back control of time.

Taking Control with Workflows

In writing this book, Pete and I had several conversations about how routines fit into planning and whether a workflow is the same thing as a routine. "Routine" is another example of how one word can carry negative emotions. You may thrive with structure and routine in your day, whereas someone else resists it because it means less freedom to go with the flow.

Pete and I agreed we like "workflow" better than "routine." Following a routine feels rigid, while following a workflow feels more flexible. So we decided to go with workflow. It doesn't matter what word you use; it's not something to fear.

A workflow is a set of regular actions, usually completed in a particular order.

We know the workbox is used when you trust it's updated with the most current appointments and tasks. The only way for the workbox to be current is if you have some kind of workflow in place to update it regularly. If a workflow is not in place, the workbox breaks down.

Creating Your ADHD Planning System

A complete planning system consists of your planning tools and the workflows required to maintain those tools, so it can be a system you trust (see Figure 7.1).

Here is how the planning system is connected:

Your ADHD Planning System

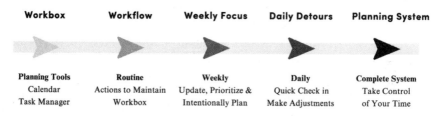

Workbox	Workflow	Weekly Focus	Daily Detours	Planning System
Planning Tools	Routine	Weekly	Daily	Complete System
Calendar	Actions to Maintain	Update, Prioritize &	Quick Check in	Take Control
Task Manager	Workbox	Intentionally Plan	Make Adjustments	of Your Time

Figure 7.1   Your ADHD planning system.

- It begins with the workbox. The two essential tools in the workbox are the calendar and the task manager. This is where your work is kept organized.
- The inboxes are a temporary holding spot for new incoming projects, tasks, and appointments.
- The Weekly Focus is a workflow that consists of collecting new information, updating the workbox, prioritizing tasks, and intentionally planning for the week ahead.
- The Daily Detour is a daily check-in to review your workbox and make necessary adjustments.
- With these four elements in place, you have created a complete planning system.

The ADHD Mind Benefits from Workflows

One of the main benefits of using workflows in planning is that you don't have to rely on your memory for how these tools work or how to maintain them. This is why I love checklists: they remember the details for you. A checklist prevents you from forgetting steps or losing track of where you are. There are several benefits to using workflows; the mission is figuring out how they work for you.

Here are a few reasons to consider them for yourself:

- **The hard work happens only once.** Workflows eliminate you having to re-create a process repeatedly. It takes some time and thought up front, but then it's done. This is why Pete and I *love* templates. You don't have to rely on memory to know what to do when it comes up again.
- **They result in better planning results.** Plans change, and it's true that it's impossible to know how long some tasks take until you do them, but that's what's great about workflows—you can estimate how long they'll take. Use the tracking guide from Chapter 4 and track the routine for only a few days. Now that you have the "real" time it takes, you can plan accordingly with confidence.
- **They eliminate distraction.** Most likely, you're already doing some kind of workflow; however, you may feel your attention is all over the place. You get distracted, forget what you were doing, start something new, and the intentions are lost. Workflows create a healthy structure to stay on task and stick with your original intention for that time.

By establishing workflows, you eliminate the feeling of having to start over again. You've already decided what to do, so you are free to focus on getting it done.

The logistics of a complete planning system requires more than one workflow. You have the workflow of the planning system, and you have two workflows inside of the system, the Weekly Focus and the Daily Detour. The next sections outline the logistics of each session.

Introducing the Weekly Focus

Because words matter, we are shedding the obligation of weekly planning and replacing it with the opportunity that comes from the Weekly *Focus*. The Weekly Focus has its own workflow that you will learn in Chapters 8, 9, and 10.

The purpose of the Weekly Focus is, first, exactly what it implies: taking time to check in on projects and prioritize tasks while looking at the week ahead.

Second, and perhaps more importantly, the Weekly Focus encourages you to approach the coming days reflectively, assigning your week an intention.

This way, even if you are challenged with distraction or schedule complications, you'll always know where to return to get started again. You may take a detour or get stuck in traffic, but you still arrive at your destination.

Scheduling the Weekly Focus Session

Deciding on when to schedule your Weekly Focus Session is not something to take lightly. This very important event can easily be ignored and forgotten if it's not planned at the right time.

Remember, systems break when they are not being used.

To set yourself up for success, be committed to the appointment and block the time as unavailable. Don't let it compete with other tasks. I recommend scheduling the session before you start the day or during a transition time, like after lunch or at the end of the day if you have the mental energy to follow the workflow.

If you miss your session, schedule for it the next day. If you have limited time, do the bare minimum. For example, review your calendar for appointments for the day or double-check your email to make sure you didn't miss something. As you practice the Weekly Focus, you will learn what this bare minimum is for you.

Follow these steps to schedule the Weekly Focus Session:

1. Choose a space to plan that you enjoy being in.
2. Choose a consistent day and time for the session.
3. Decide a time frame (30–45 minutes is recommended).
4. Intentionally plan for the session by time-blocking it on your calendar as a recurring event in your calendar.
5. Set a reminder 10 minutes before the session.

Starting the Weekly Focus Session

In my planning membership, we start the Weekly Focus session with a breathing exercise. Transitions are difficult with ADHD, and this helps to slow down the nervous system, especially if you are feeling anxious about the process. It's very simple: you close your eyes, inhale a long, deep breath, hold the breath to a count of five, and then exhale, releasing any stress or anxiety you are feeling at this moment. Repeat three times. Now it's time to get started.

Follow these steps to start the Weekly Focus Session:

1. Eliminate known distractions.
2. Display your calendar.
3. Open your task manager.
4. Gather any other planning tools necessary.
5. Display your Weekly Focus Checklist (you will create this checklist in Chapter 10).
6. Begin with your reflection.

Include Reflection in Your Weekly Focus

Besides reading this book, when was the last time you took time to reflect on how your complete planning system is working? Until now, I guess you've gone straight to blaming yourself for something that wasn't working. This is not a natural thing to do, but I learned quickly from my membership group that it's a significant step. It allows you to step back and review the complete system without making assumptions, and I hope you replace judgment with curiosity.

I recommended writing these reflections in the same place every time and refer to them when something in the system isn't working or you're feeling down and need a reminder of how far you've come. This is for you; no one else will be looking at them. Use positive language, be your biggest advocate, and know that Pete and I are cheering for you from afar.

Use the "Reflections Exercise" worksheet (**Worksheet 10** in the appendix) as a resource for probing questions *and* to track your successes. The first exercise on the worksheet is to recognize your successes from the last week.

Celebrate everything; it all matters.

It will also lead you to think about what's working and what needs attention. We do this exercise every week in the membership program. You can decide how often you want to include it; I suggest at the very least once a month for an evaluation of the system and weekly for the successes. This is how you build your confidence and self-esteem and stop apologizing for your ADHD.

I've had people tell me they could use their entire time during the Weekly Focus just on reflection. I get it, but remember the intention of the Weekly Focus is to organize the week ahead; if you want to spend more time in reflection, schedule a different appointment outside of the Weekly Focus and keep the reflection to 5–10 minutes only.

Planning Tip

If planning the entire week feels overwhelming, consider scheduling two Weekly Focus sessions to break the week into two parts. In my membership group, we meet on Mondays and Thursdays. On Mondays, we get a snapshot of the week ahead and plan for the next three days. On Thursdays, we meet to update what we planned on Monday and plan for the end of the week, including the weekends.

Missed a Weekly Focus Session?

With ADHD, consistency is not always something to depend on. What you can depend on is a complete and resilient planning system. It's different now because you see how the tools are connected. Having a piece of paper full of tasks is nothing to fear or feel scattered about. Your workflow includes these random pieces of paper.

When you notice that it's been a while since you've done a Weekly Focus Session, please challenge any limiting beliefs that may show up for you. This is nothing to feel ashamed about, and resist the urge to avoid the system or believe now is a good time to invest in new planning tools.

Now is the time to give yourself grace and get to work on updating the workbox by following your Planning Workflow. You have one now;

you didn't before. It may feel daunting and scary opening a task manager that hasn't seen the day of light in a while, but you will be OK. You know what you're doing, and you will get it done.

Set Yourself up for Success

Whenever you try something new, it takes time and practice before you can feel confident about what you're doing. The Weekly Focus is a work in progress. As you practice it, you will learn what's necessary to pay attention to and what can be delayed for a later review. It most likely will take longer at first, but soon you'll get a system down where it won't feel like a burden or another task to do. You will want to do your planning because it's what drives what work is being done that day and it allows you to take an active role in how to spend your time.

Here's what to keep in mind during the Weekly Focus:

- **Show up.** It's easy to block the time; what's not easy is showing up. Show up when you're overwhelmed and you don't feel like it, and when you do, the success for the day is the act of showing up. Don't use guilt or shame as motivators to show up; this doesn't work. Show up because you have courage and resiliency. Whatever you find, you can face. You have a trusted system now; things are different than they used to be.
- **It's emotional.** Expect this experience to bring up some heavy emotions. It takes courage to review your projects and update your workbox. You may not like what you see, but keep challenging the limiting beliefs, and remember that your to-do list does not represent who you are as a person. Keep persevering—you've got this, and we are cheering for you from afar.
- **Be patient.** Whenever you start a new routine, it takes a while to find your flow, and with ADHD, be careful not to get stuck in absolute thinking, perfectionism, and overcomplicating the process. After more practice, you'll know how long it takes to complete your checklist and can plan it into your schedule. You will also quickly learn your criteria for "good enough." Instead of ignoring the Weekly Focus, do what you can with the time you have.

- **Be realistic.** Timing is everything; I can't stress this enough. If Weekly Focus sessions take more than 30–45 minutes to complete, reevaluate your checklist. *Long sessions of two hours get ignored.* Track how long it takes to get through each step and set a time limit if you're spending too long on one step. Decide which tasks are the *must-do* and which are the *nice-to-do.* The exception is for larger new projects that entail many details and working with other people, or if you are doing long-term planning like annual, quarterly, or monthly planning. Think about how much time you are willing to spend and adjust your process to fit this time.
- **Consider accountability.** Doing this alone can be challenging, so if you are not showing up as much as you would like, find ways to be accountable, not in a shaming, bad way but in a supportive ADHD way. Accountability increases the consistency rate of showing up. Having a body double (someone who works alongside you; they can be planning or doing something different) helps you to stay on task and make it more fun. It can be a co-worker, friend, partner, or someone in the ADHD community.

Introducing the Daily Detour

The second workflow in your complete planning system is the Daily Detour. During the Weekly Focus sessions, you tentatively planned the week ahead. The Daily Detour is like the supporting actor in your movie. The Daily Detour, aka the Daily Plan, doesn't have a great reputation. Until now, you may have avoided doing any kind of daily plan. This could result from an outdated task manager, fear of what you will find, or simply forgetting to check the workbox before the day starts. You may think it's unimportant and you don't have time for it.

I want to challenge this line of thinking.

- How much time did you spend feeling bad about the last appointment you missed?
- How much time did you spend looking for that note with the important dates?

- How was your stress level when you felt unprepared for an appointment?

The Daily Detour takes 5–10 minutes.

Yes, it's true. So even if you don't do this every day, it's OK because the Weekly Focus supports the Daily Detour and vice versa. Doing the Daily Detour *most* of the time allows the Weekly Focus to be more manageable and take less than 45 minutes to complete. These workflows support your ADHD by giving you a positive structure to keep your projects and tasks organized and updated. Your planning approach has changed. Your workbox is not something to fear; it's your daily GPS. You *want* to look at it to reach your destination the way you want.

The Daily Detour is a check-in to ensure you're going in the right direction.

Plans and priorities change. Sometimes this is in your control; other times, it's not. It's nothing to take personally or feel like you failed in planning.

Take the detour and adjust to your new estimated arrival time.

Scheduling the Daily Detour

Here is how to schedule your Daily Detour:

1. Choose a time that doesn't compete with other appointments.
2. Schedule the night before or the first thing in the morning.
3. Schedule as a recurring event in your calendar.
4. Set a reminder 10 minutes before the start time.

Starting the Daily Detour

Follow these steps to start the Daily Detour:

1. Display your calendar.
2. Open your task manager.
3. Open your Daily Detour Checklist (you will create this checklist in Chapter 10).

Tips for the Daily Detour

What to keep in mind during the Daily Detour:

- **Timing matters.** If this is not the first or last thing you do in the morning, it will most likely not get done. Everything in between these hours, you've gone on with the day. OK, if you miss it, you miss it, you can get through the day without working in your workboxes, but do you want to?
- **Trust your workbox.** Use these tools the way you intended to use them. As you practice working in the systems, keep the list in front of you of which tools do what. Have your workbox displayed on the computer, write down your priorities for the day on a whiteboard, and place a bright yellow sticky note on your computer with the time of your doctor's appointment so you don't forget.

Planning Tip

Set a ritual around when you check in with your workbox; for example, at breakfast, review the day ahead; at noon, adjust for the afternoon; and late afternoon, check off completed tasks and plan for tomorrow. This keeps your workbox updated and gives you the confidence you need to feel in control of your time and schedule.

Planning Is Working

For some reason, there is a myth that people believe that organizing and planning their work is not work. They feel guilty for doing it during office hours and feel like it *should* be done on their own time. Do you believe this? If so, I want to challenge you: could this be a limiting belief?

In coaching, we are taught not to ask "why?" questions because it can sound judgmental if your tone is incorrect, and it can put the client on the defensive by having to explain themselves. I'm breaking the rules. This is not coming from a placement of judgment; it's from curiosity because I have so many questions.

Why is planning not considered work? What makes it insignificant? What are the managers and owners of the world assuming? That "work," whatever that is, just happens without any organization or planning? Do they want their employees to feel unprepared and stressed all the time? I really don't get it.

I'm not suggesting you spend all day updating your workbox and planning; there is a balance. But think of it this way: if you work an average of 40 hours per week and have one Weekly Focus session and five Daily Detours, you spend roughly 1 hour and 30 minutes planning. This is using 3% of your time. The time saved by planning will vary, but what doesn't vary are the feelings of less stress, more confidence, and more control a person feels when they have something to lead them into the day.

Working Is Not Planning

I hope you continue to question why planning hasn't been a priority until now, but I need to warn you that something can happen during your planning sessions, and it happens so quickly that you won't notice until it's too late.

Living with ADHD means distractions are going to happen, and what better distraction is an email where you think, "I will quickly respond and then get back to planning." I use this example for a reason: it's a trap to fall into, even for those who do not have ADHD.

I led a planning session in my membership program and checked my email to look for tasks to add to my task manager. I noticed a question come in, and without thinking, I started to reply; as soon as I realized what I was doing, I stopped and moved the email to my task manager to reply later. The person who asked the question was in my planning session! This is precisely what I tell people not to do and there I was doing it!

It happens to all of us, but as soon as you notice, remember the intention of the session is to plan, not to do the work. The work will get done later; your planning session only gets a fraction of your attention, so honor that time the best you can.

To ensure you stay on task, set a timer every few minutes. This will help you focus on your plan until it becomes a natural habit. You may need the timer less, or maybe not; maybe it's one of those things that support your ADHD and it's a good thing to have in your workbox.

Make It Fun

Let's face it: planning is boring, and the shine of a new tool eventually wears off; there are things you can do to make it more fun and engaging.

Here are a few ideas:

- Bring your favorite coffee or drink to the session.
- Change your location.
- Turn on your favorite music that energizes you.
- Use bright colors and images to create visual interest.
- Make it social and plan with other people.
- Check in with your accountability partner.
- Gamify the routine by using apps that turn tasks into quests.
- Race against yourself by timing tasks and then try to beat your record.
- Set up different rewards each time you finish a session.
- Change up the tools you are using (Chapter 10).

The ADHDer's Simple Guide to Not Hating Structure

My favorite routine kicks off my day. It's the routine I have around walking the dog and making my morning tea.

First, I get dressed. Well, most of the time I get dressed. Sometimes I stumble downstairs in my boxers and T-shirt. Whatever my state of repair, I move from upstairs to down.

I fill the kettle. It's a Cuisinart and has buttons that align to the proper temperature for different varieties of tea: 175° for green tea, 185° for white tea, 190° for Oolong. I am, however, a tea savage. I set the kettle for "Boil: Black" and press start.

It takes about seven minutes to boil the water, and in that time, I'm usually freezing, so I hustle back upstairs to dress. I put my earbuds in my ears and start the first podcast playing, fasten my watch to my wrist and prepare it to start an "Outdoor Walk" workout, brush my teeth and (sometimes) my hair, then head back downstairs to the kitchen.

(*continued*)

I place three Irish Breakfast teabags in a small teapot and pour the now-boiling water over it. I'm creating a *zavarka*, a deeply concentrated black tea that I'll use throughout the day.

The process of using the *zavarka* reportedly dates back to the Russian Civil War in 1917 and also to my wife's return from her experience living in Russia in 1997.

Whichever date you're thinking of, using the *zavarka* is a Russian routine that allows me to pour a little bit of the concentrate of rich black tea into my mug, top it off with fresh boiling water, and thus make immediately drinkable tea without waiting for a fresh bag to steep on each refill. I drink a significant amount of tea.

Once the small teapot is steeping, I place the harness and leash on the dog and start my "Outdoor Walk" workout on my watch. I walk the same route each day, which allows me to track my pace reliably. I notice mood swings based on trends in my pace on this walking route, and that helps me prepare for my daily attention to mental health self-care. The walk takes 31 minutes, give or take.

On return to the house, I unleash the dog. If it's wet out, he gets a thorough toweling, after which he begins his morning routine of rooting his face around adorably in the couch cushions.

I head back upstairs to shower, dress, and prepare for the day. My tea has now been steeping for about 50 minutes. I place a 2.5-count pour of Califia Plant-Based Creamer in my 24-ounce Yeti travel mug, along with two small scoops of Stevia powdered sweetener. I do not know why I settled on these two products. I don't remember when I was introduced to them. But I know exactly what they taste like together, and my entire world would fall off its axis if they were to be substituted with other products.

I have a Bodum Schiuma Milk Frother, which I buzz in the cup as I pour a five-count of tea from the small teapot. There is a bit of foam in the cup now, which is irrelevant to the routine, but I do like the look of it. I pour more boiling water over the cup to fill it to the brim for my perfect tea. I grab a Barebells protein bar from the refrigerator and move into my office to settle in for the day.

I've never written that out. There are more steps than I would have expected, and I have stronger opinions on each step than I would have thought, too. But this is the morning routine I carry out every day, Monday through Saturday, all year long. It satisfies a deeply ritualistic part of me, the part that has a strong allegiance to brands like Yeti and Califia for no particular reason other than *it's just the way it should be done.*

There is no friction for me in the process. The reason I haven't written it out is because I have never needed to do so. I have internalized this process so deeply into who I am in the morning that it is now rote.

I count on this routine just as much as I count on routines for time and productivity to help me keep my head on straight. This morning routine orients me to the day ahead. It is as much a fastidious process in and of itself as it is a tool for helping me change contexts between sleeping and waking that is less cognitively jarring than just falling out of bed and landing in front of the computer. A routine that eases me through otherwise crushing context changes is a routine of extraordinarily high value to me.

High value, low friction. That's the mantra.

When you head out of your bedroom and you make your way to wherever it may be that you do the work that pays for your shoes, that is the mantra I'd like to ask you to consider. Because it won't be long before you run into your first routine of the day. You're a landscaper, and you're putting your equipment into your truck *just so.* You're a lighting designer in a theater, and you're coiling your cables and tying down rigging *just so.* You're a line cook. You're a cleaner. You're a bookkeeper, a lawyer, a teacher, a cop; you do your job *just so.* Why?

(continued)

(*continued*)

In the beginning, you were likely taught to do it the way you do it. Maybe you learned it in a classroom. Maybe you learned it on YouTube. Wherever you got it, you internalized the way you did because some other resources told you to do it that way. That's how all our routines start. It's terrific, too, that we have this natural mechanism between us as humans to be able to transfer knowledge, skills, and abilities to one another.

I'm going to say this next thing so that you know that I know that we agree on a fundamental thing about the ADHD brain, and then we can move on.

The ADHDer doesn't truck well with routines.

What a relief to get that off my chest. You probably think I'm nuts, right, Jordan? Going on and on about my tea routine, this thing I cherish in my day, without talking about how routines are hard? I get it.

We struggle with consistency. Doing the same thing every day is easy for a little while, then we fall out of the habit or get bored. We crave novelty, stimulation, and excitement. In that craving, we forget steps in established routines because our working memory stinks. We don't like it when people tell us what to do—in this case, "people" also refers to "my calendar"—and we resent them for it. At the same time, having an accountability partner remind us what to do from time to time is the only way we can get things done.

We're a beautiful confusion, Jordan, a neuro-radical puzzle wrapped around a fidget spinner.

High value, low friction, remember? The reason my personal tea ceremony works so well for me day after day is that it *doesn't*. Surprised? About four months ago, had we gone through this exercise, you would have heard me describe an equally meticulous *coffee* ceremony with different equipment, different timing, the works. Over time, the value of drinking too much coffee decreased as my gut discomfort increased, and I was inspired to change my routine.

The act of change was glorious and overblown in the most ADHD-forward fashion. I tried different *everything* and drank far too much tea to be productive along the way. But when I found the new routine, I knew two things: this new routine would work fine, and eventually, it would need to change again.

We take it as axiomatic that routines must evolve. We must question their function and purpose because what works today may not work tomorrow.

We inherit process bloat, which turns invisible to us over time, costing valuable time that could be better put toward new endeavors. Plus, we have ADHD. Reviewing old processes for opportunities to change can be *fun*.

I have an electronic work system—my *workbox*—in which I have built project templates with tasks and subtasks for everything I do. Producing an episode of a specific podcast, for example, might include 15–20 separate tasks leading from planning through recording and ultimately delivery into the podcast directories. I produce so many shows each week that you might think that I wouldn't need such a detailed level of task definition to produce a show. What I've found is that the more shows I produce, the more careless I can be about completing every step in the process.

Without the checklist, I miss things.

To ensure those project templates retain their value, I have a separate reminder for each that prompts me to review them step-by-step every six months. Do I need every step of the process? Have I changed systems somewhere along the way and forgotten to update the checklist to account for it? For example, last year, we changed hosting providers. Over the course of two weeks, we moved over 7,000 individual podcast episodes from one provider to another, which called for new and different steps for me to release new episodes going forward. In just a few minutes, I was

(*continued*)

(continued)

able to cement into practice the results of the continuous testing we performed by editing those templates and creating a new foundation for production going forward.

Routines require learning through trial and error.

Our ADHD brains will retaliate against that learning process. This doesn't mean a focus on routines isn't valuable. In fact, it makes them even more so. Think about it, Jordan: routines aren't just there to help you remember to put toothpaste on the brush before you brush your teeth.

Routines are how you engage with the world around you. They remind you to make calls, pay bills, and engage with your peers at work or your friends at home. Routines are the currency of productivity exchanged and amplified through culture.

Doing your part means you have to adapt to some routines and create some others while always asking yourself the most important question: *why am I doing it this way?*

Coach's Corner

Nothing like turning old beliefs about planning and routines upside down! I hope this chapter inspires you to open the doors of opportunity and see what happens when implementing these ideas. I think it's important to emphasize that your destination is more than a completed to-do list. Sure, it feels good to cross things off, but you know what feels even better? It's that you no longer have to apologize for who you are. You begin to feel differently about your schedule, tasks, and life. There are many other ways to measure your success than how many tasks you complete.

I hope you take time to notice the subtle thoughts and reframing that unconsciously are happening. Maybe you recovered from an ADHD moment quicker than you used to. Maybe you asked for an extension on a deadline. Maybe you started a project that you've been avoiding without judgment. Maybe you called someone you've been wanting to call, and instead of feeling guilty or ashamed, you were grateful for the reconnection. Instead of assuming something will go bad, you ask yourself, what if it goes well? Maybe you decided to apply for the job. Maybe you were OK with rescheduling a task in the future. Imagine what it will feel like to come back to the workbox and see it as a friend whom you haven't seen in a while but are so grateful for, and you have the kind of relationship that it doesn't matter how much time has passed; you appreciate and support one another.

There are so many maybes, just waiting for you. There are many things to celebrate, recognize, and acknowledge; no more brushing them off to the side. You are transforming into a confident planner who works with ADHD and knows you're worthy and valuable in the world.

Chapter Summary

The following are the key points from the chapter:

- Vehicles need gas to run and workboxes need attention.
- Words hold many emotions and expectations. Choose ones that support you.
- The workbox contains the planning tools; this is where your work is kept organized.
- Workflows are the actions taken when a new project, appointment, task, or idea arrives.
- Workflows are made up of routines—the same set of actions done on a regular basis to keep the workbox maintained.
- The Weekly Focus gives you a snapshot of the week ahead.
- It will take 30–45 minutes to do our Weekly Focus session.
- The Daily Detour redirects your focus when needed.
- Timing is everything, otherwise the sessions don't get done.
- Planning is working, but working while you are planning is not recommended.
- Make the routines fun and engaging.
- Questioning and evaluating your routines is supporting your ADHD.

In Part 3, you will create a customized planning workflow checklist. This checklist will outline the steps to enter new projects and tasks, how to update and prioritize what's most important, and finally, how to intentionally plan to create a life designed by you.

It's starting to come together. Let's dive into the next part to put the finishing touches on your complete planning system.

PART
III
The Planning Workflow

HERE YOU ARE, in the final part of the book. This is the last piece for completing your planning system. Let's review where you've been so far. In the book's first part, you learned about ADHD and how it impacts you personally. We challenged the limiting beliefs and got closer to radically accepting ADHD. The second part focused on building your workbox, choosing tools that support your ADHD, and building a workflow using the tools as one system instead of separate entities.

This part focuses on creating a Planning Workflow that maintains your workbox. The next few chapters center on keeping your workbox a trusted system *and* focus on how your life is more than a to-do list.

The Planning Workflow consists of three steps:

1. Capture and Collect (Chapter 8)
2. Update and Prioritize (Chapter 9)
3. Intentional Planning (Chapter 10)

This is the Planning Workflow you follow during the Weekly Focus sessions. As you go through each chapter, you will customize what action steps you will include in your Weekly Focus and Daily Detour Checklists.

The final chapter will explore what to do when you notice your planning system isn't working and how to connect long-term planning to your weekly focus.

Let's begin!

8

Step 1: Capture and Collect

CAPTURE AND COLLECT is the first step of the Planning Workflow.

The Planning Workflow

Capture and Collect	Update and Prioritize	Intentional Planning
• Capture new appointments and tasks into inboxes • Collect during planning sessions	• Update calendar and task manager • Prioritize tasks for the upcoming week	• Decide what to time block • Schedule into the calendar • Set reminders

Imagine your desk is covered with sticky notes and random pieces of paper that could potentially have important information. It's not too hard to imagine, is it? Because we are all guilty of it. The solution seems simple: just put your important information into your workbox, and you won't have to worry about this problem. Really, is it that simple? No, it's not, and this book is about how to support your ADHD, not set you up with more unrealistic expectations.

The first step of the Planning Workflow is to capture and collect any tasks, appointments, thoughts, and ideas that have been generated since the last time you did a planning session. These items get captured in your inboxes. Just like a new email lands in your inbox, these inboxes work similarly. When a new task comes to you and, for whatever reason, you can't put it into your calendar and task manager, you can place it here temporarily.

Planning Tip

On days when you feel scattered, unorganized, and unsure of what to do next, don't wait until the next Weekly Focus to capture and collect your tasks. Take a few minutes to check your inboxes and transfer the information to the right place. There is a great sense of relief when you're not afraid you are missing anything.

Determining Where You Need to Collect

Review all your planning tools from the workbox and identify which ones will be used as an inbox. List each inbox on the "Inbox List" worksheet (**Worksheet 11** in the appendix). For each inbox, write out the workflow (actions you will take) to get the new information into your workbox. Figure 8.1 shows an example of the "Inbox List" worksheet filled out.

Inbox List

Inbox	Workflow
Task Manager - Inbox	Review new tasks and assign them to areas and projects. Add details like due dates, labels, etc.
Email	Check email for new tasks. Enter into task manager inbox and sort into correct areas and projects.
Text Messages	Review past text messages from the last few days to make sure I didn't miss any new tasks or changes in appointments.
Notebooks	Review notebooks for new tasks and information I need to capture and collect.

Figure 8.1   Sample "Inbox List" worksheet.

Include checking each of the inboxes during the Weekly Focus and Daily Detour. The inboxes are temporary, and the sooner you can get them into the main workbox tools (calendar and task manager), the less scattered you will feel.

A History of Inboxes

I have a lot of inboxes. I bet you do, too. For me, the journey started in high school when my parents sprung for my own phone line to my bedroom, which came with—you guessed it—a voicemail box. That was the first time I experienced full ownership of an inbox in which outsiders could reach into my life and leave me their thoughts across the moat around my house. It was so exciting.

I did all the great voicemail games. I'd read passages from my favorite books as my outgoing message or I'd say, "Hello, this is Pete," as if I'd picked up the phone, then I'd wait 30 seconds and say, "Just kidding. You got my voicemail!" So annoying. The best one, in my humble opinion, was when I mimicked Laurie Anderson's "O, Superman" and sang my outgoing message through a knockoff vocoder. Thanks to lame recording in my landline phone, I had a full year of callers not understanding a single word I was saying.

What I know about that first inbox, the voicemail inbox, is that I listened to every single message that was ever left for me.

I went to college and got a new voicemail inbox, plus my first email inbox with it. I was officially living in the future and, once again, pledged to read and interact with every message sent to me. Such was the bleeding edge of inbox technology.

Things changed quickly. I went from having voicemail and email to IRC messaging, ICQ, AOL Instant Messenger, and MSN Messenger, all *before* the year 2000. The last 15 years have brought more options for new service inboxes like WhatsApp, Kik, Facebook, Snap, Telegram, Twitter, Signal, Mastodon, Instagram, and Discord. That's a big tech *brand salad*, I know.

(continued)

(*continued*)

But the important takeaway is that if you're a user of any—or all—of those services, each one of them gives you a new inbox.

So that we have a clear definition of terms between us:

An inbox is any container of incoming and unprocessed information.

Naturally, we've been talking all about your digital inboxes, but your plain old dead-tree inbox falls in the same category; how you process your incoming mail falls right in line with your inbox strategy.

What are your inboxes?

Jordan, if I asked that question before you read this book, I'm pretty sure I would have gotten the same glare and nasty look as when I asked what systems you currently use. It's different now because even though this may be a new concept, you've already done half the work to find your answer. You did it when you chose your tools. After you read this chapter, you may want to add a tool or two to the toolbox; who knows?

Where do *new incoming* projects and tasks live in your world? Here are a few possibilities:

- Communication boards
- Emails
- Voicemails
- Text messages
- Notebooks
- Planners
- Journals
- Postal mail

The Brain Dump: The Last Great Inbox in Your Head

I was first introduced to the term *brain dump* in the 1990s, and it had nothing to do with productivity at all. Back then, in my circles, a brain dump was all about transitioning a project from one person or team to another. A brain dump meant, "Tell me everything you know about this thing you've been working on so that I can take over as if I've been working on it with you all along."

Beyond that, the etymology of the term is a touch mysterious. It's enough to make me wonder if the originator of the term might not be all that proud of what they hath wrought in terms of scatological productivity humor. According to Google's Ngram Viewer, the thing took off in productivity circles in the mid-'90s, and the term has been used in many productivity systems under other monikers. Whatever language you use to frame the concept, the result is largely the same: take everything floating around your head and document it somewhere.

It sounds stupidly easy, doesn't it, Jordan? And it should be easy. It should be the easiest thing in the world.

It. Is. Not.

See, the neurotypical brain is an engine for this stuff. Ask my wife for a list of things taking up her attention and drawing focus from what is right in front of her, and that's what you'll get: a perfectly bulleted list of activities. Then she goes on about her day.

The ADHD brain? That's a horse of a different color, Jordan. When you ask your ADHD brain to come up with a list of things drawing our focus and attention in different directions, your brain promptly walks into one of those clear booths with a fan on the floor blowing dollar bills around. Except the dollar bills aren't dollar bills at all. They're ideas. They're tasks. They're all the things taking up our attention that should rightly be on a list. We have to chase them, grab at them as they blow around us wildly. Sure, we'll catch a few before the fan turns off. We'll feel great about ourselves as the rest of the little slips fall to the floor around us.

Suffice it to say, we'll never quite catch them all, and our confidence isn't always to be trusted.

The ADHD Brain Dump

As Pete pointed out, the brain dump is different for the ADHD brain. You won't catch every idea, and it certainly will not come up as a perfect bullet list of activities, and that's OK. You will feel temporary

146 Unapologetically ADHD

relief but not for long because now you have a long list of things to do and ideas to sort. This is where other people get stuck because, without a system in place, the list doesn't go anywhere, and there is no trust the list will even be looked at again, let alone be a productive piece of paper.

You don't need to worry because you have a planning system with tools specifically to hold the information you just dumped. I think *brain dump* is a horrible name. But the purpose of it serves the ADHD brain well.

It allows you to unload at least some of the heavy burden of keeping track of too many ideas, things, concerns, worries, memories, tasks, beliefs, feelings, and anything else that's going on.

This exercise with a horrible name allows you to get racing thoughts out of your head and onto paper (or a screen) to process without so much distraction; notice I didn't say "without *any* distraction." (ADHD support for the win!) Use the "Brain Dump" worksheet (**Worksheet 12** in the appendix) for this exercise.

Set a timer for any amount of time and write down whatever comes to mind without any filter or judgment. This exercise can be a part of Weekly Focus and Daily Detour checklists if you like, but it can also be done anytime you feel overwhelmed. It's often the first thing I recommend when a client is stressed over a new project or an event that is to be planned; it's a good starting point for breaking projects down to see them more clearly.

The Inboxing Game

To make any of this inbox stuff work, you need to think about it as a *practice*.

That means that it's not a thing you do, just making lists willy-nilly around your house. You're not a sticky note wrangler, after all. Making it a practice means that giving some attention to your inboxes becomes a part of who you are. You are an inboxer, and you might just become the heavyweight inboxing champion of the world.

A person who makes inboxing part of their identity is a person who can't help but become more thoughtful and introspective. They grow to relish the idea of examining their activities and obligations. A daily reflection on what is floating around in their head leads to an examination of the importance of those things at a core level.

This is a person constantly asking, "Is this thing important enough to who I am that I will document it, retain it, and carve the time out of my life to take some action on it?"

If the answer is yes, then that thing is granted passage from the inbox to the workbox. There's a practical benefit to making inboxing a practice, of course. There will always be more tiny slips of ideas floating around your brain that you can't catch in any one session. *Transforming this from an activity you do once in a while into a routine ensures that you'll capture more of the things floating around your brain each day that you missed the day before.*

That is why I like the process of inboxing so much. It doesn't matter how far I stray from my process or how many days go by when distraction pulls me in directions unrelated to the work of my life. When I return to the process of disgorging activity from my various inboxes and committing it to my workbox system, I'm reminded of the major activities that matter to me.

- What do I do for others?
- What do I do for my family?
- What do I do that I love?
- What do I do for fun?

"Pete," you're saying. "I have ADHD. I can't just capture everything that comes into my head and every message that comes into my messaging apps. It'll be a never-ending list, and I'll just end up feeling terrible about it." I hear you loud and clear, Jordan. And you're right. You're creating a pretty significant list if you write everything down.

But here's the magic lever you get to pull for any task, any time: **writing it down is not a commitment to do it.**

(continued)

(*continued*)

Go ahead and read that again because it might be the most important thing to internalize about inboxing after "do some inboxing" in the first place.

The act of committing the things in your head and your inboxes into your working system is your commitment to yourself that you won't forget those things.

What *future you* chooses to do with those items once it comes time to sit down and work is a mark of freedom you'll get to celebrate later.

Going from Inbox to Workbox

I love that Pete has us read this statement two times: *But here's the magic lever you get to pull for any task, any time: writing it down is not a commitment to do it.* Now you've read it three times! (Another win for ADHD!) Indeed, we don't have time to do everything; we need to make some hard choices on what is most important right now. You will learn more about prioritizing in Chapter 9.

The things that matter now need to be transferred from the inbox into your workbox. I wish I could tell you magic is involved, but sadly it's not. The information gets transferred because you make it happen because you, my friend, have a workflow to follow.

Some inboxes will be easy to transfer; you collect the random sticky notes, enter the information in the workbox, and recycle the paper. This inbox is checked off. In my experience, I have found two inboxes to be particularly difficult to find a consistent workflow to feel like you have control over the transfer of tasks. These inboxes are Emails and Notebooks (really any kind of paper like a notepad or spiral bound).

Emails

Let's set the expectations upfront: this book is not about organizing email. However, many tasks and invites come through email, so we can't ignore this important and common inbox. Many of you probably use your email inbox as a task list. I'm also willing to bet you that you have tried different methods of organizing email by using flags and different folders.

Our focus is on getting the action items out of your email system and into the workbox. I don't expect that what I am recommending will work for everyone. You will either adopt the idea, adjust it in some way to fit your needs, or ignore it altogether. This is true for any of the strategies we share with you in this book and specifically for your Planning Workflow.

What's different now is that you have a workbox, a complete planning system of elements that work together. This means you no longer have to use your email inbox as a task list, because you already have one in your task manager (the one you trust).

Here are a couple of ideas on how to get those moved to a trusted workbox.

Create a Mail Folder Labeled Calendar   The idea for this folder is to move any emails that contain appointment requests, updates, and cancellations into this folder. This way, they do not live in your inbox with every other email you've received and get missed. You may think your email is not organized enough to make such a bold move, so why create another folder to the side that will get ignored? I get it; this is not my first rodeo, so let me tell you more before believing any limiting beliefs that may be showing up for you right now.

I worked with a therapist who has her own practice, and she consistently receives emails from potential clients about booking and canceling appointments. Because her email was disorganized and piled up (you're not the only one!), we decided to use this strategy to see what would happen.

So she created a new workflow. This workflow was specific to how she sorts and processes client emails about appointments. She created the *Calendar* file folder and dragged any new email to that folder whenever she received scheduling-related messages. But the workflow doesn't stop there. If she had time, she immediately added the appointment to the calendar, but as you can imagine, this *time* doesn't often occur. As a safety precaution and to support her ADHD, she added a daily reoccurring task: Check Calendar Email. This was the reminder she needed to make sure the emails were responded to in a timely manner. This eliminated a stressor she had endured for years. Imagine this for you—it's worth trying.

Create a Mail Folder Labeled *To Do*   The idea for the *To Do* file is similar to the calendar. Any emails with a task or some kind of action or reply needed can be moved to this folder. Again, it takes it out of the inbox and into a separate file folder, which will be easier to manage. This strategy, particularly for tasks, has the potential to get overcomplicated. I've witnessed many people get hung up on the details, which stops them from trying the strategy.

My best advice is to keep it simple, ignore the what-if scenarios, and practice the strategy. Think about your current organizational system. Why do you flag one email over another? Predetermine what "to do" means to you. Is it for when you need to reply to someone? Or is there a task that someone is asking you to do?

The end result we are looking for is to get the new information out of email and into your workbox. If you want to stop using email as your to-do list, practicing this strategy will help you do that.

Move the Email to Your Task Manager   The other option is to move the email directly to your task manager. Here we get to the heart of why we use the term *workbox* to describe the tools we use to get work done. Your email inbox is a mess of unrelated clutter. But moving email from your client into a workbox tool allows you to focus on work while working, freeing yourself from the distraction of email noise.

This strategy works beautifully with digital systems because you can move the email with the calendar appointment and/or a task attached to the email to your task manager; it's like magic. The two systems need to connect, so make sure to learn how to do it within your own system, whether that's with a drag-and-drop or keyboard shortcut.

You can do this when you open the email; it takes seconds. In many workbox tools, you'll find you have a second layer of inbox, a place to log tasks as they come to you for processing later, and the email-to-task system shortcuts will normally put email in that second inbox. To process the email out of the inbox, add it to your weekly and daily planning checklists.

Both strategies are two steps and require reminders. This is why the checklists and workflows are important—because remembering to do this in the middle of a busy day is not happening, but when you support your ADHD and set up *trusted* systems to remind you what to do, you can also let go of the stressor you've endured for years.

Notebooks

Notebooks or any piece of paper become inboxes, whether intended to be or not. This strategy makes them intentional and frees you from worrying if you will lose them later. To avoid having too many pieces of paper where potentially important information might be hidden, designate one notebook (single capture point) for ideas, thoughts, and tasks in one spot. When you update the workbox, cross off what you've entered to avoid confusion.

Another idea I've helped clients adopt is having different notebooks for certain meetings or work. For example:

- Team meetings use the green notebook (labeled)
- Supervisor meetings use the blue notebook (labeled)

The workflow is to collect the tasks from the meetings into the workbox, and the notes for reference are moved to the note-taking system (see Chapter 3). If this is part of your process, add it to your checklists.

Workboxing

I'll be honest, I started calling it "workboxing" because I'm not much of an athlete and the idea of incorporating the allusion to boxing into my day makes me laugh.

What we're really talking about is working—just plain and simple nose-to-the-grindstone work. The beauty and the twist of workboxing come in what you're not doing while you're getting your work done.

(continued)

(*continued*)

First, when you're workboxing, you don't have to look at your inboxes. I'm not so pedantic or unrealistic to think you can do all your work without your inboxes open and active sometimes. But if you've made inboxing a practice, you don't have to think about them while you're working if you don't want to.

You have the power and the agency to close your email for a while, to put your phone on Do Not Disturb, and get some work done. If you need to keep your email open, you can do that. But you don't have to. You can give yourself the freedom to reduce distraction, find focus, and do it without feeling like you're going to be punished for forgetting one thing or another.

Oh, I'm sorry, you've never felt like that? Like you spend 101% of your time wondering what you've forgotten to do while you're doing something else? You must be reading this book because you're a *fan* of ADHD then, right? That's fine. We welcome all brains!

There are those in the productivity biz who recommend reminding yourself to check your email and assorted inboxes during a dedicated session. For example, you might sit down at your desk at eight in the morning, process your email, and close it up again to get to work. Then, around lunch or four in the afternoon, you come back around and do it again. No shame in that. I've tried it. I know people for whom it works gangbusters.

It doesn't work for me because I don't have the sort of career that allows it. I spend a lot of my time creating podcasts, and when I'm standing in front of a hot microphone, you'd better believe my inboxes are closed. As a result, when I'm not on the mic, I have to spend a little time processing incoming work from my inboxes into my workbox.

In case you have forgotten, I still have ADHD. That's right, I haven't solved it since I started contributing to this book. As a result, writing all these essays is a nontrivial challenge for my fireworks brain. As I'm writing this dumb sentence, all I can think about is my buddy who just got a new computer and is managing his transfer from his old computer to his new one with a cable that I loaned him. I'm writing it for you here because that's on my mind, and I need to check on him to make sure it's going all right and find out when I need to come by and get my cable.

Option-Command-A. That's the keyboard shortcut on my computer that opens the "Quick Add" box from anywhere I might be working in my system, ready for me to type. So I did that: Option-Command-A, "Check in with C on the transfer and get the cable back before he tries to steal it," Return.

That's it. I took the thing in my head, put it in my system in a matter of a few seconds, and the moment I hit return on my keyboard, I was back to writing this sentence. I entered an item of work for later at the moment I was thinking about it. Before it was able to take hold in the form of hyper-focus, I documented it and dismissed it, freeing my attention to return to writing.

Now, I don't *have* to think about it anymore. If I had been recording a podcast, I could even pull this little trick in front of that hot mic. Whatever I'm doing, I know it's in the system, and the next time I'm reminded to look at it, it's going to be there. I can focus on my work, my writing, my podcasting, whatever.

Creating Permission for Whatever Comes Next

I don't like to brag, but I know a *lot* of people with ADHD. Here's a thing I've noticed about the lot of them, apart from the fact that they're a *good hang*: They share a wildly unpredictable routine for checking their incoming signals.

The point of Inboxing and Workboxing is not to solve the problem of unpredictability. You might always be unpredictable, leaving your voicemail or texts on read for weeks.

The point of the dynamic duo of inbound processing is that you have a trusted process.

You know that when you do look at that voicemail, if it involves a task, then you know exactly where to put it. And you know that when you do have the time and attention to sit down

(continued)

(*continued*)

and look at your workbox, you know that you can trust that doing the next thing on the list is fair game. You have permission to do the work free of distraction from everything else if you're ready for it.

People overthink processes like these. Every single day is another day to judge ourselves for not living up to another productivity expert's process.

If you stop to think about the true atomic component of any productivity system, it's this: do you know what to do next?

I ask myself that question because, for me, it's all about managing the incoming signals and funneling anything related to work into the workbox. Sure, I layer some scheduling and prioritizing on top of it. But if you're struggling with overload, it might just be time to strip your process to the bones and ask yourself that question, too.

Drafting Your Workflow Checklists

It's time to start drafting your Planning Workflows for the Weekly Focus and Daily Detour Checklists. At the end of the next three chapters, please decide which actions you want to include on your checklists by using the "Planning Workflow Builder" worksheet (**Worksheet 13** in the appendix). At the end of Chapter 10, you will create checklists for each workflow.

Review the chapter and decide what tasks you want to add to your checklists. The actions for Capture and Collect are the same for the weekly and daily routines; the only difference is the time you spend. If you've missed a few Daily Detours, then this step will take longer to catch up for the Weekly Focus.

Here are the action steps for Capture and Collect:

1. Scan the area for new information and collect it into one spot.
2. Review inboxes for new information.
3. Enter new information into the workbox.

Coach's Corner

Step 1 is completed! I hope you start to feel the benefits of having systems and processes in place that support your ADHD. You are building something flexible and resilient. It's OK not to add tasks to your workbox immediately; you have several inboxes to choose from. We aren't saying to throw away the sticky notes; include them because what's different is they serve the purpose of being a temporary holding spot until you can enter them into the workbox. When you begin to see how these tools work together, it's not so overwhelming because now you are planning with your ADHD in mind.

Chapter Summary

The following are the key points from the chapter:

- Identify your inboxes.
- Brain dumps are helpful to clear your mind.
- Remember, just because it's written down doesn't mean you are committed to doing it.
- Enter tasks from the inbox into the workbox during the Weekly Focus and Daily Detours.
- Begin drafting your version of the Weekly Focus and Daily Detour checklists.

It's a feeling of relief when your important information is safe and sound in the workbox, but there is more work to do. Time is a limited resource, and decisions need to be made. In the next chapter, we are exploring another P word: prioritizing. It sounds horrifying, I know, but don't give up yet, because what if there was a systematic way to prioritize? A flowchart of sorts that could guide you to making decisions quicker? That's an interesting idea. Let's go find out!

9

Step 2: Updating and Prioritizing

WELCOME TO STEP 2 of the Planning Workflow.

The Planning Workflow

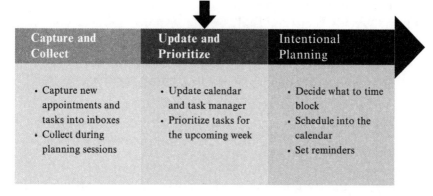

Capture and Collect	Update and Prioritize	Intentional Planning
• Capture new appointments and tasks into inboxes • Collect during planning sessions	• Update calendar and task manager • Prioritize tasks for the upcoming week	• Decide what to time block • Schedule into the calendar • Set reminders

In step 1, you captured and collected new appointments and tasks from your inboxes. Now is the time to enter them into the workbox, update your other projects and tasks, and prioritize what is most important to do this week. This seems like a scary chapter, I get it. Who has time to update? You're thrilled that all your tasks are in one spot! Yes, this is a success for sure, and I know prioritizing is a P word that hurts when you read it. But this is the thing: I want you to get uncomfortable. Why?

Because discomfort means transformation and change is on the horizon.

Updating the Workbox

If it's been a while since you last visited your workbox, you might experience some heavy emotions like shame, disappointment, frustration, and so many limiting beliefs. My guess is there will be a lot of *I should have* thoughts crossing your mind. Your old way of dealing with these emotions was probably to avoid the workbox altogether and then, later down the road, try again with something new. My hope for you is to be kind to yourself and remember that whatever you find, you can handle. Challenge your limiting beliefs and remember that the workbox is only a set of tools; they are not judging you, and they are not a representation of who you are as a person.

Our workbox has a job to do, and that is to tell you what to do. For it to do a good job, we need to update it with the most current information. It will be easier to maintain the more consistent you are with the Weekly Focus and Daily Detour sessions; however, don't fear, because your complete planning system supports your ADHD. So even if it's been a while, you are covered.

Here is a step-by-step process to update your workbox *anytime*:

1. Add new appointments to the calendar.
2. Cross-reference and update calendars if you have more than one.
3. Add new projects and tasks to the task manager.
4. Add important information like due dates, tags, and subtasks.
5. Check off completed tasks.
6. Review and update current projects and tasks.

Planning Tip

One of the ways to keep your task manager updated is to have it open during the day while you're working. As you complete a task, be sure to check it off. If new information comes in that needs to be added to the workbox, and it's open, you'll be more likely to enter it at the time. Keeping your workbox open like this decreases the amount of updating that needs to be done during Weekly Focus and Daily Detours.

Updating Without Shame

It's frustrating to open your workbox and see overdue tasks. One client referred to them as *cascading tasks* that pile up on one another until everything is buried. The common solution is to find a new tool. This has been the solution for most of your life, but is it really a solution? Before we jump to conclusions, let's explore the factors leading to cascading and overdue tasks.

Avoiding Cascading Tasks

Cascading tasks occur when tasks have the same due date. They become overdue when the tasks don't get done. This pile of tasks gets bigger if you don't review and update the due dates. The tool has nothing to do with this problem. Remind yourself and stay strong: shift your focus away from evaluating new tools to finding a better method for working with due dates in the tool you have.

To get out from under the cascade, adjust the dates:

- Prioritize red tasks first, the ones with real deadlines this week.
- Identify green tasks, the ones with no due date or those that are later than this week.
- Review your calendar and only allow one or two tasks to stay; reschedule the rest for a later review. (Note: You will soon understand the difference between the red and green tasks.)

Rescheduling tasks in your workbox is not a failure.

You have not failed, and the workbox has not failed. It simply means priorities shifted. Reevaluating what's most important and what can wait is part of updating the workbox. Speaking of priorities, let's learn about how to set them.

Knowing the Difference Between a Due Date and a Review Date

Due dates are confusing. Is this a real due date or a fake one? It's like setting your clock ahead 15 minutes, thinking this strategy prevents you from being late. The problem is you know it's fake. You know deep down inside, you still have 15 minutes.

The same magical thinking happens with due dates. We think if we put a due date on a task, it somehow will make us want to do the task. It's urgent, right? It's due today. But it's not really due today. Just like the 15-minute strategy, it doesn't really work.

In the next section, when we discuss prioritizing, you will learn that red tasks are reserved for the tasks with real due dates this week. We don't create fake due dates in our systems; instead, we use review dates with a tentative due date that can change at any time.

A real due date is the date a task is due.

For example, a term paper is due on March 30. Rent is due on the 1st of the month. Your proposal is due on February 1. The slides are due on Friday. You need to clean your house before Saturday evening, before guests arrive for a dinner party. These are all real deadlines.

Many tasks in our lives do not have real due dates. For example, work on the website, exercise, research vacation spots, clean room, and write a blog post. This is where it gets tricky. Most of my clients attach a due date because they don't want to forget the task. The priority of the task is not considered. The tasks don't get done and they pile up because the due date means nothing. It's just a shameful reminder of your high expectations. Do you see what's happening?

Cascading tasks are not a tool problem; they're a due date and prioritization problem.

I want to introduce you to the *review date*. The review date is not when something is due.

The review date is a time to review the project or task and decide where it fits into your current priorities.

If it meets the criteria to be prioritized along with other active projects, then set the dates accordingly. Give yourself permission to take these tasks off your daily and weekly lists. They are only cluttering it up and hiding the tasks that are most important right now.

You no longer need to worry if a project or a task will be forgotten, because you have a workflow around updating and prioritizing your workbox. The review date is scheduled, so it will get back to you for review. It's only out of mind temporarily until it's time to review again.

We do want to create a workflow around review dates that work best for you.

For example, any task with a review date will be dated on the 1st and the 15th of the month. Expect that on those two dates, the number of tasks on your *today* view will show up. Intentionally plan for these reviews on your calendar as a recurring event. Not every project or task has to follow this rule; some projects don't need to be reviewed for a few months. Date them as you see fit.

Planning Tip

Workboxes have different methods of working with due dates; some systems allow a start date and end date, and some only give you the due date option. You don't want the task to show up only on the due date, because then it's too late. The solution is to get creative with task descriptions! It's perfectly acceptable to write tasks that include "Review" in the title. In other systems, you might choose to create a tag for "Review" and surface those tasks on a given review day. You get to work with your own system and decide the best way for you to know when to start working on a task and how you want to define what your system's "Due" date means. If the feature of duration dates is important to you and you do not have them, consider adopting a new tool that better supports your ADHD.

The Impact of ADHD and Prioritizing

How does a person plan their day if everything is important and urgent? This feels like fact, but it's simply not true. You could even say it's a limiting belief. Can everything really hold the same value? Have you ever noticed how emotion can determine if a task is completed? Sometimes this has nothing to do with the importance of the task. You may have a productive day but then realize you've been busy all day but not on the right things. This may be why emotion drives your actions.

Logically, you know the truth, but with ADHD comes emotional dysregulation. These emotions often drive your limiting beliefs. This is a heavy burden to carry, but the good news is that awareness sparks change. You have learned how to challenge those beliefs (in Chapter 1, in case you forgot). It's time to say goodbye to shame, blame, and the "should" of to-do lists.

Who Are You Lying To? Priorities, Procrastination, and Self-Deception

I learned pretty early in my relationship with my ADHD the importance of prioritizing the work of my life. I demonstrated it repeatedly by not prioritizing at all and enduring the result, which was generally full of chaos and shame, followed by a string of apologies and promises of "I'll be better next time." We should probably talk about that a little bit, and then we can reflect on the big question that Compromised Pete keeps in his back pocket to give a bit of perspective while hopefully dodging the repeated maladaptive behavior part.

I have one question that I ask myself that plays a role across a variety of situations in which I am asked to produce work but have prioritized poorly. If we were sitting together, Jordan, at a café in Paris, for example, talking about our respective ADHD strategies, I might lean in at this point and look at you intensely in the eyes. You would look away because this is a very uncomfortable action for me to take. I would say, "Look at me, Jordan. Look me in the eyes." You would do so, probably a little scared, and I would ask you the question: "Who are you lying to, Jordan? Are you lying to me? Or are you lying to yourself?"

I remember the first time that question was used on me. I was working in a newsroom and had been tasked with taking a camera and a truck and capturing footage of extreme close-ups of sleet and snow falling on an overpass. This footage would be used as the chromakey background behind the local weather map for the weather segment of the ten o'clock news broadcast. I didn't have a strong feeling about the assignment.

This was the problem. As a result, I spent the bulk of the evening doing everything but the assignment given to me.

There was some drama. When I had been asked 1,500 times for the footage, I had yet to leave the station to capture it. I went to the rack of camera gear, and to my complete surprise, there were no cameras left and no trucks to drive. I missed the opportunity to do the job I'd been asked to do.

I found the assignment editor and had a full sermon complete with all the reasons the footage wasn't there. It wasn't my fault, there were no trucks, the cameras were all signed out, the weather wasn't cooperating, and on and on and on. After what felt like a minute of my rambling, he interrupted me.

"Who are you lying to right now?" he asked.

"I don't . . ." Pete stammered like a buffoon, ". . . I don't understand."

"Are you lying to me, or are you lying to yourself? Because back when I assigned the story to you, there were plenty of cameras and plenty of trucks. You chose to do other things up until the time that we need those things for"—I remember a distinctly pregnant pause here before he said—"the *news.*"

That didn't feel great, Jordan. I was a kid, practically, and the passive-aggressive dressing down pissed me off. Then it turned to some pretty hardcore rejection with a heaping side of depression topped with a soupçon of anxiety that I would never amount to anything at all and that my burgeoning career was over.

But that *question*, Jordan, was incredible for me. I felt like the assignment editor had seen through the veil of all my distractions, all my procrastination, all my fruitless efforts to prioritize my afternoon and replaced them with the sting of truth. The answer to the question wasn't easy to swallow, either. Was I lying to him or to myself?

Both, of course.

This is another paradox of ADHD. Setting priorities is the thing that unlocks waves of potential acceleration toward an area of focus in our lives. At the same time, those very priorities are the source of ammunition with which to shoot ourselves in the foot.

Think of it another way. Have you ever taken a class in which your teacher performed some action that they had taught you not to do? Artists break the so-called rules of painting or sculpture all the time. Great writers sling punctuation hither and yon. That's because one of the axioms of expertise is that you must first learn the rules in order to break them.

(continued)

(*continued*)

The same applies to prioritizing. Once you learn how to prioritize your work and obligations, you have the freedom to change the rules to fit your life best. With ADHD, the power to change the rules can serve to give you even better excuses to lie to yourself and others, just as I did to my assignment editor.

If I'd been living in truth at that moment, I would have told him that I used every excuse that I could think of and volunteered for every passing job suitable for an entry-level photographer and editor because I couldn't get my brain engaged in a task I felt was silly. I knew well that he had told me how to prioritize my afternoon, and I rebuilt my schedule to serve my other interests.

My brain happens to be exceptional at wielding the skills of prioritization—and reprioritization—to paint new stories and rationalizations supporting the choices I make. In the end, just as my assignment editor noted, the stories are just that: flimsy rationalizations justifying my own inability to trust my own brain.

Nikki has a robust process for prioritizing the work of your life, and doing it according to your values. What I hope you'll take from my aside, Jordan, is that you could be working in a newsroom like I was, or you could be a teacher, a bus driver, or a veterinarian. Everyone gets tied in knots with responsibilities and obligations they don't know what to do with, regardless of profession. It's been 30 years since that engagement in the newsroom, and it still happens to me more often than I care to admit.

So what happens now? What happens when I cheat my priorities and let my fractured focus get in the way of my responsibilities? I fall back on that one question that provides reflection and perspective. "Pete," I ask, "Who are you lying to now?"

ADHD Priority Checklist

Sometimes in life, we want people to tell us what to do so we can avoid making decisions. I'm not here to tell you what to do; I can't prioritize for you. However, I can create a set of guidelines to help you find the answer, and that is exactly what the ADHD Priority Checklist is for you (see Figure 9.1).

The Priority Checklist

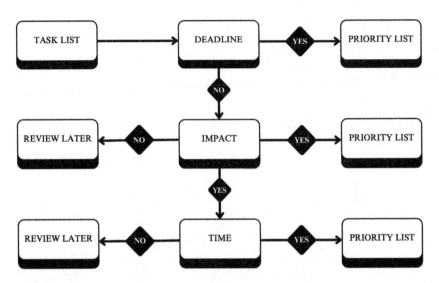

Figure 9.1   The ADHD Priority Checklist.

There are three qualifiers to consider when prioritizing using the ADHD Priority Checklist:

- **Deadline:** The first and easiest way to determine the importance of a task is the deadline. This does not include fake deadlines. If it's a true deadline this week, it moves to the priority list.
  - o Tasks with no deadline, or with deadlines more than two weeks out, move onto Impact.
- **Impact:** Next, consider the task's impact on yourself and others. Consider both negative and positive consequences; the more at stake, the higher the impact.
  - o High-impact tasks are moved to the priority list.
  - o Medium-impact tasks move onto Time.
  - o Low-impact tasks move to review later.
- **Time:** Review the calendar to see how much time is available to work on the tasks from the priority list. You may need to adjust to ensure the time to work on the tasks. Intentional planning ensures you have time to work on the top priorities.

o Top priorities are scheduled first.
o If space is available, schedule one or two medium impact tasks.

Review later tasks are dated in the future to decide on later.

Zero-Based Budgeting for Time/Function

Did you pick up the book today with a hankering for a story about the younger days of Corporate Pete when he still wore a *suit* to work every day? This, Jordan, is your special day because I have for you yet another fiscal metaphor for your ADHD success.

I used to work for a small consulting company with big clients. So there were just a few of us who had to deliver services to those clients while also running the firm. That meant limited resources in terms of both budget for new projects and limited time spread among those of us who had to do the work. None of that is new for you, I bet. You have too much stuff to do and not enough time or money to do it. "Tell me something I don't know, Pete."

To keep the business moving forward, we relied on a process called zero-based budgeting (ZBB). *Wait!* I know, I know, you read the word "budget" and ran for the hills. But seriously, hear me out. This might help you.

A standard budget, if you're a lovable budgeting nerd, starts with the assumption that you're going to spend about the same in the coming period as you spend the period before and invites you to make adjustments to those assumptions in planning. This includes ongoing operations and expenses, too.

Zero-based budgeting starts with no assumptions whatsoever. Everything starts at zero, even ongoing operations.

We would begin our planning session with our sales assumptions. How much revenue would we be able to confirm for the coming six months? With that number, we're able to begin accounting for ongoing operations and new ideas.

I'm going to continue writing about this in terms of young Pete wearing a suit and going through the zero-based budgeting process. But it's important that you recognize that this whole thing is an allegory. It's really a story about how we should all be working with our own limited time and cognitive resources and that we all have a budget that, when exceeded, causes us to fall completely to pieces. Do you see that? About the allegory? Let's keep going.

In a normal year, actual and projected revenue would comfortably cover ongoing operational expenses and after we would write all those items on the foreboding barren plain of the Flipchart, we would begin our individual presentations.

A ZBB presentation allowed each of us to stand up before one another and make a pitch for something *new*. Maybe it would be for a new piece of software. Maybe one of us was pitching for some continuing education or certification. Maybe we needed a new chair in the waiting room. Whatever the pitch, we had to have answers for the following points:

- Cost: How much will it cost?
- Schedule: How long will it take, and when will funds be required?
- Performance: What is the objective? What is the end result of successful funding of the new project, and how will success contribute to the growth of the organization?

This is a brutal process. Like, root-canal-on-a-city-bus brutal. I'm laid bare, presenting my personal aspirations and attempting to make the case that my idea is somehow better than everyone else's, and I'm judging myself along the way, too. Because if I'm pitching a project like ongoing education and it doesn't get picked, what does that say about *me*? Is the rest of the team saying that I'm not good enough or smart enough to make use of more education? Are they saying my value is in filling a cold space at a table and nothing more?

Of course they're not. And once I get through the presentation process, I get to see it in action. The whole team takes in the

(continued)

(continued)

entirety of the presentations and rank-orders them all on that Flipchart. By the end, the once-blank paper is now full of an ordered list containing all the work of the company for the next six months.

And it turns out the presentation wasn't the hardest part after all. As we're sitting there, looking at the list of all the new projects we're excited about kicking off in the new period, our CEO walks over with a red pen and draws a line. Everything above the line stays. Everything below the line goes. Such are our resources for the period.

This is the gladiatorial combat of budgeting. Maybe I won, and my project was funded. I'm celebrating, but not too happily. Because others are just sitting there, watching as new ideas, the ideas that might fuel them, energize them, get cut to the floor. Sure, they could pitch again in six months. But things change, needs change, and many of these ideas lose their luster when the sparkle of currency goes dim.

As much as I write about the zero-based budgeting process with a bit of drama, I loved it. Here's why:

We can't do everything.

We have ADHD, so we *think* we can do everything. We can't. We don't have enough time, money, attention, or support. Sometimes, we're the ones who have to draw the red line.

As hard as it is, the red line is a gift. Once I know all the things I want to do and look soberly at that list of desires next to a calendar, drawing a red line becomes the liberating stroke of future accomplishment. Whether I'm assessing my day, week, month, or beyond, once I know what I'm not able to do, I have the freedom to turn all my available resources toward the things I *can* do.

Externalizing Decision-Making Can Be a Good Thing

I don't know about you, but sometimes, when I'm compromised, I'm not good at letting things go. I count on my wife to keep me grounded. I count on my clients and partners to keep me pointed in the right direction. And sometimes, when I get myself lost in a long march toward an uncertain horizon, I need someone to tell me that things no longer serve my best interests.

That's what the zero-based budgeting process taught me: a fixation on my own pitches was a distraction and largely an act of selfishness once the decision had been made. It turns out I also needed a process to count on to tell me when to let go. Comparing my upcoming interests and passions to a zero-based reality does that perfectly.

Self-Awareness Is a Practice

When it's used well, zero-based thinking removes assumptions and forces me to align activities to the resources I have available. Once I start to see myself in this light, I begin to recalculate what it means to have resources. I start to calculate attention and focus. I am able to see where I'm overextending myself or neglecting important areas of my life.

My daughter calculates her internal resources in *spoons*, a unit of measure coined by Christine Miserandino to describe the emotional and cognitive experience of living with Lupus and handling daily life. I love spoons. It's just a word, but it's a word with weight once I attach it to my own reservoir. The Flipchart of the zero-based budget represented dollars and cents at the office. But for me, every item on the list can be calculated in the spoons I have left with which to complete them.

Success Is Double-Edged

What happens when I really do see my project sit *above* the red line? That's the mark of a successful pitch and should be an occasion of joy and opportunity.

It turns out that Compromised Pete can spin this experience right into the guardrail with little to no effort at all. The moment of accomplishment is met with the moment of awareness that a new journey has begun. It's the journey of the imposter.

(continued)

(*continued*)

Take the "zero-based" part out of the discussion for just a moment and think about how much you love to think about your goals. Probably not all that much, right? Goals—any goals—are easy reminders of past failures. When Compromised Pete steps up to the plate with all the hope of hitting a home run, he's standing right in the position of past strikes. "I've never achieved my goals in the past, Pete," you're saying, "So why would I be excited about the opportunity to fail at new goals now?"

There's nothing to be excited about when it comes to confronting demons. It's dark and terrifying to stare at the compromised part of myself and speak to him in a way that he'll understand. I'm angry. I'm confused. I'm frustrated that the compromised part of me has been in the driver's seat. I want to yell and scream at him, tell him to back off, sit down, and get out of the way.

When was the last time you carried that kind of rage into a conversation with a friend or family member and had things go all right? *Rhetorical Question Engaged.*

The compromised version of me is angry and confused, too. He's been with me all along, cataloging all the times me and my ADHD have missed a meeting or a school pickup. He sees all the clutter in my house that has gone invisible to me over time. He still sits in the very current feelings of insignificance from those times I was put on a performance plan at work, passed over for a promotion, or laid off entirely. For the compromised version of me, the version of me living deep inside, there lives an accounting of every loss the two of us have lived. My ADHD might let me lose myself from time to time as I dive into hyper-focus on something engaging, but the other me is never able to forget.

Yelling at the part of me who is in pain, pointing that rage inside, is an act of cruelty, Jordan. It only leads to more pain, which is hard to hear, I know, especially when you're feeling compromised yourself. This brings me all the way back around to budgeting.

There I am, sitting in that conference room, seeing my project approved above the red line. I'm shocked, afraid, and a little disappointed that the buildup to the pitch only leads to more work, which I'm not confident I can do.

There's a pat on my back. People are standing up and milling about and I'm hearing "Congratulations," and it appears to be directed at me. These people, my co-worker, are coming to me and shaking my hand. They are encouraging me, expressing their excitement for whatever comes next. They are expressing their confidence in their own vote and in my ability to do the job they have entrusted me to do.

Such is the double-edged success of the zero-based budget. You become the rational executor of your untapped potential through the lens of your available resources.

Double-edged success is still a success. For me, thinking about my available time and energy as my resources, and working each day to balance those resources with the work in front of me, helps me to make clear and intentional choices.

Either/Or . . . Both/And

I know budgets aren't sexy. And maybe hearing the story of a dummy like me learning a process for budgeting that would later become a model for living is more of a nuisance than an illustration for you. I do hope it's the latter, but just in case, here's one final thought experiment that comes from this exercise.

In that long list of priorities, we're forced to make choices. We can do this thing or that thing, but when we make that choice, we move on.

Or do we? In my experience working through zero-based activity scheduling with folks, we discover that our ADHD brains are able to move pretty fluidly between states when we figure out what our attachment is to the activities on our lists.

We can be traditionalists and explore our lists from the place of "Either/Or," or we can be maximalists and explore our lists as "Both/And."

Either/Or planners see one thing at the expense of another. "I can't take the cat to the vet and get my car registration renewed

(*continued*)

(*continued*)

on the same day." Either the cat or the car, not both. But is it possible for you to capture the energy of wanting to see your cat live a long and healthy life *and* continue to drive your car legally?

What if you attempted the risky maneuver of taking the cat to the vet and then dropping by the DMV for that pesky registration on the same trip?

Shocking, I know. And it's ridiculous because the DMV would never issue a registration to a cat.

The gift of the zero-based mentality for me is that it illuminates opportunities to practice elasticity in the mundanities of life. I learned to appreciate how strongly I feel about my commitments as I make an effort to reprioritize them.

Finally, when I stop to think about my ZBB list, I'm able to shake just a bit of the ADHD clutter from my mind as I remember that the act of making the list was a courageous act of planning and a fearless effort to free my mind of the things that I don't need to think about in favor of those I do.

Introducing the ADHD Priority Matrix

If you've ever read a productivity book, you've probably heard of the Eisenhower Matrix. It's built off a quote, possibly apocryphal, that has been widely attributed to Dwight D. Eisenhower himself, spoken referring to having heard it from another unnamed college president: "I have two kinds of problems, the urgent and the important. The urgent are not important, and the important are never urgent" (Eisenhower Matrix, 2017). That was the quote that launched a thousand self-help ships.

It was adapted into a concept that categorizes all your work into four quadrants.

- **Quadrant I:** Urgent and Important. These are tasks you do first.
- **Quadrant II:** Not Urgent but Important. These are tasks you schedule for later, which are generally thought of as supporting long-term vision.

- **Quadrant III:** Urgent but Not Important: These tasks are screaming for your attention, but they do not contribute to your long-term plans and are perfect candidates for delegating.
- **Quadrant IV:** Neither Urgent nor Important: These are tasks you delete.

This sounds good until you get to tasks you delegate (Urgent but Not Important). This is complicated for ADHD because the difference between urgent and important is often blurred. To avoid confusion, I created the ADHD Priority Matrix (Figure 9.2), which transitions from four categories to three and uses color to differentiate the categories.

- Red = Important and Urgent: Schedule this week
- Green = Important but Not Urgent: Schedule this week or later
- Blue = Not Important and Not Urgent: Review later

Here's how the ADHD Priority Matrix breaks down:

- **Red tasks:** These are your top-priority tasks that are due this week and are intentionally planned. Red tasks are not to be feared; we all have red tasks. It doesn't mean they are late; they just need your attention.
- **Green tasks:** These tasks are not due this week and may not have a due date. They are important and help you be proactive with your work. If you have space on your calendar, choose one to two greens to schedule after the red tasks are scheduled.
- **Blue tasks:** These tasks will be reviewed later. They are not a priority right now, but you don't want to forget about them (for example, planning a vacation or special event). When they come up, you decide if you want to move them to a green or red task or continue postponing for later.

Delegating and Deleting Tasks

The ADHD Matrix simplifies the original process; however, delegating and deleting tasks are still positive ways to prioritize. Delegation is a great strategy to harness your strengths and delegate where you feel the most challenged. Don't be afraid to ask for help. This may be uncomfortable initially, but think about how much time it frees up to focus on what matters most. Please delete tasks from your workbox that are no longer relevant—this can be one of the first decisions made in the update step.

The ADHD Priority Matrix

Red Tasks: Important / Urgent
• Last-minute emergencies • Overdue tasks • Tasks that may negatively impact someone else if not completed • Creates a positive outcome with great benefit to you and/or others • Self-care (sleep, meal times, exercise, medical appointments, etc.)

Green Tasks: Important / Not Urgent
• Due next week or in the near future • Tasks without a scheduled deadline • Quick, simple tasks; an easy "win" • Proactive scheduling (future appointments, meetings, etc.) • Personal/Social (hobbies, meeting with friends, etc.)

Blue Tasks: Not Important / Not Urgent
• Someday/maybe ideas • Tasks with a far future deadline • Reading or research that interests you • Important dates in the future (birthdays, holidays, vacation, etc.) • Extra clutter on the list ("Do Later")

Figure 9.2   The ADHD Priority Matrix.

> **Planning Tip**
>
> Color code tasks by the priority color. In digital systems, add a red, blue, or green emoji tag. In the paper system, use colored pens or highlighters. When updating your tasks, identify when the tasks need to change color.

Learning to Disappoint Others

Casey Dixon is an ADHD coach and happens to be a friend and a regular guest on our podcast. She shared a strategy that resonated with me. She asks her clients, "Who can you disappoint today?" (Dixon, 2022). It's a shocking question for the ADHDer. Still, Casey's point is clear: instead of inadvertently disappointing others through negligence or fear, figure out how to communicate clearly and authentically that you cannot satisfy a particular prior agreement. In doing so, you are purposely disappointing and freeing yourself of the shame, stress, and burden of rejection they carry.

On the show, Pete was inspired. "It's the RSD [Rejection Sensitive Dysphoria]!" he said. "This is like looking square in the eyes of RSD and saying, I'm going to own it. I'm going to own it today on my terms. I'd rather disappoint you than have you passively be disappointed in me."

Prioritizing Tips

There will always be exceptions where the Priority Checklist and the ADHD Matrix will not help you know what to do next. The following are some common situations with a few ideas on how to get closer to your answer.

Avoid Looking at All Your Tasks at the Same Time

Your master list of projects and tasks is not a daily to-do list. Use the Priority Checklist shown in Figure 9.1 to zero in on the most important tasks for the week and then by day. Look at these tasks separately from everything else. What that number "should" be is debatable; practice prioritizing first and learn what feels right to you.

Someone Else's Emergency May Not Be Your Emergency

This is a lesson I learned from Pete: just because a new task comes in during the day doesn't mean it automatically becomes a top priority. What? How often have you checked your email and felt the need to respond immediately, even if you were in the middle of working on a top priority? For me, all the time! When you catch yourself doing this, pause, evaluate where it falls with the other tasks, and decide when it will get your attention.

Lower Your Expectations

This is the hard truth: your expectations are too high, time is limited, and there is not enough time in the day to get everything done. Is this a limiting belief? No, it's not. It's a limiting belief to think you can. Instead of setting yourself up to fail, set yourself up for success. The pace at which you get things done will vary; this is part of living in the ADHD Time Zone.

Drafting Your Workflow Checklist

Review the chapter and add the action steps you want to include to your "Planning Workflow Builder" (Worksheet 13 in the appendix). During the Weekly Focus, you will be updating and prioritizing the workbox for the next week or at least the next few days. You will review all current projects and adjust where needed. The Daily Detour is only looking at today; it's a quick overview of the workbox.

Here are the action steps for Update and Prioritize:

- Add appointments to the calendar.
- Cross-reference and update calendars if you have more than one.
- Add new projects and tasks to the task manager.
- Add important information like due dates, tags, and subtasks.
- Check off completed tasks.
- Review and update current projects and tasks.
- Review tasks by using the ADHD Priority Checklist.
- Color code tasks by using the ADHD Matrix.

- Identify your priority list tasks.
- Update due dates and adjust the review dates of tasks.

Coach's Corner

Logically, we know that not everything has the same urgency, but it doesn't feel like it when emotions get in the way. With these tools and ideas on updating and prioritizing, we hope to give you a new perspective, so the next time you feel like a million tennis balls are being thrown at you at the same time, you have a resource to filter out what's most important.

This chapter is one to read a few times. Your brain is so accustomed to living in stress and anxiety that it's hard to imagine anything different. Yet that is precisely what we are asking you to do because it can be in your control.

This book is not about how to do more in less time; it's about understanding and supporting your ADHD. Let go of the high expectations and allow yourself to be you, not what you think you should be. Life will not get any less busy, time will remain limited, prioritizing continues to be challenging, and hard choices will need to be made, but they are *your* choices to make. Take back control of *your* time.

Chapter Summary

The following are the key points from the chapter:

- Updating is not scary; it's part of maintaining a workbox that works.
- Due date and review later are different concepts.
- It's OK to reschedule and review tasks in the future.
- Priorities and circumstances shift.
- The three key factors to prioritizing are deadlines, impact, and time.
- The ADHD Matrix is a different approach from the Eisenhower Matrix.

- The ADHD Matrix uses a color-coding system to identify the urgency of the task.
- Delegating, deleting, and disappointing others are valuable considerations in prioritizing.

You are so close to completing your complete planning system—can you feel it? Are you hopeful and inspired? We sure hope so. The next chapter is the last step of the Planning Workflow, where the actual planning happens, when your calendar meets the task list. Is it a marriage made in heaven, or more like a War of the Roses? Let's find out!

10

Step 3: Intentional Planning

CONGRATULATIONS ON MAKING it to the final step in the Planning Workflow, which connects everything you've done so far into a plan of action.

The Planning Workflow

Capture and Collect	Update and Prioritize	Intentional Planning
• Capture new appointments and tasks into inboxes • Collect during planning sessions	• Update calendar and task manager • Prioritize tasks for the upcoming week	• Decide what to time block • Schedule into the calendar • Set reminders

Intentional planning (aka *time blocking*) is scheduling time on your calendar to work on a specific project, task, or set of tasks.

But before getting into the ins and outs of intentional planning on a weekly and daily basis, I want to bring you back to your personal data summary and review your intentions and reasons for reading this book. I strongly believe life is more than a to-do list.

Your to-do list does not define who you are and is not worth tearing down your self-esteem.

I had a conversation with an ADHD mom who was really struggling and felt like she was failing in everything she was doing. I asked her if her kids knew she loved them, and she said, "Yes, of course." When I asked her if there was anything more important than that, she responded, "No, there's not." I see this repeatedly—people beating themselves up and putting too much value on their lists. Unless it's a life-or-death situation, the list does not need to be done today. It just doesn't.

It's time to set aside these unrealistic expectations and make time for what really matters to you.

The Purpose of Intentional Planning

We want to have time for what matters and still have time for the things that need to get done. At the end of this chapter, I hope you find that list to be smaller as you lean into prioritizing and having realistic expectations, rather than those that were made from ideas of what you *should* be.

Intentional planning allows you to structure your day on your own terms.

As you will soon learn, every hour of your day does not need to be scheduled, and not every task needs to be planned. This may work for a day or two, but the plan will quickly get interrupted, and because ADHD is so prone to all-or-nothing thinking, you may feel the entire day is ruined.

When there's an intention behind a time block, it means something; you decided this is a priority and needs your focus at this time. You can always change your mind, and this is in your control. Many people tell me they always react to what's in front of them, whether important or not. If you have blocked time, it gives you time to get back on track.

A magical thing happens with intentional planning: time blindness gets glasses.

When you look at your task list of 25 items to do today, look at your calendar and see the three appointments scheduled, all of which require travel time, guess what happens? Time blindness puts on a pair of glasses and sees this isn't possible. This is not a limiting belief; checking off the 25 items and attending all three appointments is impossible. This means going back to step 3 and prioritizing the 25 tasks. What must be done *today*? I'm willing to bet that maybe one or two things might be a must, but the others can wait; the key here is not to blame yourself for not getting it all done. It's not your fault; accept the day as it is and move on.

We've asked you to reframe everything you know about planning and it's no different here. It's time to *believe* you have control over your time.

How Do I Find the Time to [Fill in the Blank]?

This question is asked often, and the answer is anything but a clear one. It depends on so many factors. What do you want to do? How many things are on your list? How much time do you have? What are you doing with your time now? What's been the roadblock to getting it done? You get the point—it's not a simple question. Plus, let's add in the potential that some of the things you want to do may, in fact, be things you think you *should* do.

I read a book that shook me to the core. It was a harsh reality but a true one. In the book *Four Thousand Weeks: Time Management for Mortals* by Oliver Burkeman, he writes, "Assuming you live to eighty, you'll have had four thousand weeks."

Let's sit with this concept for a moment.

This means you have roughly around 4,000 weeks of living. I'm already on the second half of that number. I know one week goes by really fast for me. How about you? This is a good time for us to radically accept that time is not guaranteed and is limited no matter how many weeks we have left.

And just in case you're hoping for the day to come when you are all *caught up* to work on *that* one project, you can guess what I'm going to say next: it's not coming. In his book, Burkeman talks about having to make hard choices because the reality is that we do not have time to do everything we want, need, or should do.

He says, "Once you stop believing that it might somehow be possible to avoid hard choices about time, it gets easier to make better ones" (Burkeman, 2021, 3).

Let's circle back to the *should* items on your list. How often do you feel guilty for not doing something you think you should do but don't really want to do, but everyone makes you feel like you should still do it? What if you would rather do something else but don't do it because you should be doing this other thing? But neither thing gets done. It's a frustrating cycle, right?

When Pete and I were talking about this concept, we used reading as an example. I'm pretty sure you will not find any research that says reading is bad for you. In fact, you're more likely to find research about how good it is for you. You have people in your life who love reading, so you think you should love reading and make it a personal goal to read more. Even though deep down, you really don't care if you read any more than you do right now. Plus, you attached the act of reading to a goal, a goal that reminds you of everything that you are not doing. Again, it's a frustrating cycle, right?

The question of how to find time to [fill in the blank] is answered by intentional planning.

Intentional planning means scheduling an appointment to work on [fill in the blank]. It isn't guaranteed; you already know many things can go wrong. However, it still increases the chances of getting done more than waiting for someday to come along. You've set the intention and set the time aside. To do this, you must be willing to give up what you did before, but this is not a bad trade if it's important to you.

What would you do if you could find one hour per week to [fill in the blank]?

Seeing the Forest for the Trees

Think about the ADHD brain with this familiar metaphor: seeing the forest for the trees. Some people see the forest but can't focus on the individual trees. Some see the trees but can't conceive of the forest in which they live. The ADHD brain sees all, the forest *and* the trees. When your focus is fractured, you can see how planning time to do [fill in the blank] can be difficult. How do you choose what to do? We know we need to make hard choices about time (thank you, Oliver Burkeman). What if we started by eliminating the ones that have "should" in front of them? Does this help make your priorities any clearer? Probably not. You need more help figuring this out. We've got you covered.

Choosing What to Plan

Choosing means prioritizing. However, let's be clear: you already prioritized your weekly tasks for the week. This is a different kind of prioritizing. This answers the question of finding time to [fill in the blank]. These choices include downtime, rest, restoration, hobbies, social connections, vacations, exercise, mental well-being, or cleaning the garage.

Here are a few things to consider:

- **Review the Wheel of Life Exercise.** Worksheet 5 is a great visual aid for assessing your current time usage. What area would most impact you if you invested more time and energy in it? What projects or activities are associated with that area? What changes are needed to free up more time for it? What can you do less of to make room for what you want?
- **How much time do you have?** Review your current schedule and decide how much time you will protect for this activity or project. Notice that I say protect because it's important to remember why this is important to you. Consider what you might have to give up making time for it. Are you willing to do so?
- **Make your decision.** At least for now, you can change your mind; you can do whatever you want; it's your time, that's the beauty of it. But at least now you can look at the trees in the forest and not feel obligated to find time for the whole forest.

Intentionally Plan for the Week

Now we turn our focus on the ins and outs of planning intentionally for weekly tasks. I hear many mixed reviews about planning intentionally; many say it doesn't work for them. They never do what they say they will do, or they can't time block because they don't know how long something will take them. This is usually when I ask them to give it another try, but let's change the approach.

Intentional planning is very similar to breaking projects down. It's a strategy that gets talked about; you learn what it means and then are told to do it. If breaking down projects is not intuitive, intentional planning has a slim chance of success without more guidance. For intentional planning to stand a chance, you need to consider your personal data summary and understand how ADHD impacts you. Until now, you most likely have not considered these things. You may have created an ideal schedule or one you should have. You know that is no longer the situation; you have a new way to plan.

Now it's time to plan differently to get a different outcome.

Real Talk: You're Already Blocking Time, You're Just Doing It Like a Chump

I don't get it, Jordan. There is this sentiment out there that time blocking doesn't work for people with ADHD. I call bunk. So in this brief essay, I want to talk a bit about what time blocking is, why it's such an incredible tool, and why I think people have the wrong idea.

Nikki has already told you what time blocking is in the planning process. As a concept, it's pretty simple: assign time to action. That's it. That action might be an email you have to write. It might be a trip to the grocery store. It might be going to sleep at night, for crying out loud. You can block any action against the time you have to do that thing.

We all already block our time. We do it so effortlessly that we don't even call it blocked time. Do you get up and take a shower in the morning? Do you do that at roughly the same time every day? Maybe you follow that with a nip of fruit or a stop by Starbucks for that almond milk, no-water chai tea latte? You probably have some time in your head there that you'll be in some sort of transport for your commute, too. If you do any of those things with the time you have in your day, you're blocking your time. Call it whatever you want, but that time is blocked.

And if you already do it, especially when you don't know you're doing it, why would anyone have objections to trying to do it with a little intention, too?

Here are a few of the objections I've heard:

- My ADHD doesn't allow me to stick to a schedule.
- I lose motivation once the novelty has worn off. I can't stick to it.
- I can't estimate the time it takes to do the things I'm blocking time to do. Stuff takes too long and I give up.
- I get too many interruptions. My job is constantly interrupting me, and I can't build a schedule in my environment.
- Too restrictive and overwhelming! It feels too rigid and compresses my creativity!
- I can't shift between tasks in blocks.
- I'm overly optimistic in my scheduling and cram too many things in each block. I feel terrible and give up.
- I hate being chained to my calendar. It constrains my freedom.
- No accountability.

Wow. Yeah, I guess it does feel pretty overwhelming, especially reading all those objections right in a row like that. Easy to get down on yourself and give up. I guess time blocking is the worst, and maybe I'll give up too. Oh, well . . . (cue the symphony of sad trombones).

Are you kidding me? Of course we're not giving up. And I'm going to give you a free pass to try it again with a single bit of advice.

First, we need to talk about *hyper-scheduling.*

Hyper-scheduling is a variant of time blocking that asks that you do, in fact, schedule every hour of your day in an attempt to meticulously account for all time spent on activities down to the minute. Before you ask—yes, that includes breaks, meals, and sleep when taken to the most extreme.

Some people need this sort of calendar. Think about people working in professions heavy with client billing, such as attorneys, consultants, support teams, or project managers. If you have to track your time to get paid, you have an incentive to track *all* your time.

(continued)

(*continued*)

The practice of hyper-scheduling bled into productivity circles thanks to Cal Newport and his book *Deep Work*. In it, he elaborated on the concept of time blocking and with it a particularly hyper-scheduled perspective. "We spend much of our day on autopilot—not giving much thought to what we're doing with our time. This is a problem. It's difficult to prevent the trivial from creeping into every corner of your schedule if you don't face, without flinching, your current balance between deep and shallow work, and then adopt the habit of pausing before action and asking, 'What makes the most sense right now?'. . . It's an idea that might seem extreme at first but will soon prove indispensable in your quest to take full advantage of the value of deep work: *Schedule every minute of your day*."

Many high-profile practitioners in the productivity influencer space have discovered Newport's style of time blocking and swear by it. We're going to sit here and be happy for those people while we get back to our ADHD brains.

Hyper-scheduling is not our target, and it's important that we separate our assumptions around time blocking from the realities of hyper-scheduling.

We're not trying to track every minute. We're not trying to account for fixed estimations of time to do a task. We're not even saying that you have to finish the task you started in a time-blocking session.

So here's the free pass, presented to you in a three-step process titled "Pete's Personal Process for Time Blocking."

1. Observe that you have some things to do.
2. Block some time for doing those things, and commit to doing those things for the amount of time blocked.
3. Do the things.

That's it. There is no trick. All you have to do is . . . well, have things to do, make time to work on them, and then work on them.

So why is it so hard? A few reasons:

- First, when people hear the term, their throat closes right up. It's terrifying because it comes with this assumption that you're blocking time to do a specific thing, and if you don't finish that thing at the end of your time, you've failed.
- Second, the calendar is already a horror trope in the mind of the ADHDer. It's easy to find it out of date, and that simple reality presents a roadblock: how can you possibly block time if your calendar isn't current?
- Third, time blocking is over-personalized. Your ability to accomplish tasks in time blocking becomes a personality test. We hate tests.

In reality, time blocking is designed to offer a modest structure while maintaining flexibility.

It provides a platform for structure and routine to practice focus. There are no requirements for the duration. Sit down for five minutes one day and an hour the next. The only obligation you have to yourself is that if you have things, you are committing to the time to work on them.

I say there is no requirement for duration, and I stand by that. But we do have a practice that we love, and that is the popular Pomodoro technique for time management.

If you're looking for a little more structure in your structure, grab a timer and try this.

1. Set a timer for 25 minutes and get to work. Usually, we'd focus on a single task in that time, but if you have a bunch of little tasks to knock out, have at it.
2. When the timer goes off, stand up and stretch. Walk around. You have 3–5 minutes.
3. At the end of the little break, come back and set the 25-minute time again.
4. The cycle repeats.

(continued)

(*continued*)

After four Pomodoro cycles, take a bigger break, 15–20 minutes. Play a game, get a bite to eat, walk around the block, or do whatever it is that you need to do to take care of your brain.

The beauty of a Pomodoro is that you find yourself in a tick-tock routine. You no longer have to think about the time passing because the timer is doing that for you. All you have to do is turn the dial, put your head down, and see what happens next.

In a bit, you're going to close this book and go on about your day. You might look at your calendar and wonder what you could do to make the first change, push the first domino over that would lead to the chain reaction you need to build more protected time into your life. Whatever you do next, think about your schedule not as time blocked, but as time shielded. You're holding up a barrier to the world as an indicator that your time is precious, and you're moving through it according to your values. You are not working in service of the work you should do. You're shielding your time so that it serves the best work you intend to do.

A very special tip of the hat to our own ADHD community moderator Bryan Brunelle, whose gift for savvy one-liners is second only to his aptitude for sending the perfect GIF in our chatrooms. He took to this concept right away and wears "I'm time *shielding*, not time *shoulding*" like a badge of honor. He promises to share that badge if you want in on it.

We have to talk about margin.

Why is this so important? Why do we care about protecting time in our schedules to do the work we deem most important and aligned with our values? If you're not already sold, then we have to talk about margin.

Imagine a box. It's just a plain, old, empty box. Start filling the box with smaller blocks of various shapes and sizes. Each of those smaller blocks represents an obligation or commitment on your list. If you're like I was, it won't be long before the box is full to overflowing, blocks pouring all over your imaginary table.

That's probably pretty easy to imagine, isn't it? We're all overcommitted. That's what we do. But we can do something different. So let's shape our metaphor. Instead of picturing all we have to do in our lives filling the box, imagine what would happen if we never let the box get more than three-quarters of the way full. What would we do with that excess capacity?

That excess capacity—what is referred to as *margin*—is the invisible space around your schedule. It's your excess capacity with which you live the undocumented parts of your life. What do you do with your margin?

- You get a full night of sleep, many nights in a row.
- You eat regular meals on a routine that fits your health, not your work, and you eat it from a plate, not a wrapper.
- You read books, plural, because reading rejuvenates the spirit and improves your capacity with language in all other areas of your life.
- You walk, ride, or climb more, relishing the full breadth of your glorious human body and all you're capable of.
- You play more games.
- You're more patient in traffic.

And, if you could not care less about any of these reasons, this one should hit home: when emergencies strike, you have the capacity to be present for those you love.

The biggest issue I find when ADHDers first explore shaping margin into their lives is fear. We struggle with empty space. There's a bittersweet balance between the desire that we have to free ourselves from the constant movement between activities and the discomfort that comes when we finally do.

Why am I talking about margin in the middle of an essay covering the wonders of time shielding? Because this is the tool you wield to begin to chip away at overcommitment, leading toward commitment. Make no mistake; this is a reclamation project, recovering calm from disorientation each day. It takes patience and practice, but it is achievable.

(continued)

(*continued*)

The moral of our time-blocking journey is this: if you don't like it, or if you haven't tried it because you know someone who complained about it, give it another shot.

This time, though, relax. Think about the rules you might have applied to your blocked time before, and let those go. They're feathers in the wind, my friend. All you have to do to make it work is have stuff, block time, and work on the stuff.

Now, go take a break. You've earned it.

Where Time Blocks Work

Not every task needs to be scheduled. Pete did a great job describing the difference between hyper-scheduling and time blocking. We are looking for something in the middle, a happy medium, so when you look at the calendar, you have a plan that makes sense, not a cluttered ball of colors with blurry words. My job is to help you find the right balance for you. Figure 10.1 shows an example of a weekly schedule. It includes different tasks and activities that work well for time blocking.

Here is an explanation for each time block with examples of what tasks may fall into these categories.

Personal Time

I think we made it pretty clear at the beginning of the chapter that intentional planning is not only for productive tasks; in fact, I want you to plan your personal time *first* before you plan anything else. Yes, you read this right; humans do an awful job of caring for themselves. Does this feel uncomfortable? You're not alone, but it's a good uncomfortable. You are taking back control of your time.

For example, if exercise is important to you, intentionally plan three days a week to go for a run. If social connections are important, have a monthly standing date with your friend every first Monday of the month. If you want to read more, plan 30 minutes every Sunday, or don't and decide to go to the dog park instead. Another option is to block off four hours every day to do whatever you want to do. Forget

Weekly schedule

TIME		MONDAY	TUESDAY	WEDNESDAY	THURSDAY	FRIDAY	SATURDAY	SUNDAY
7	00							
	30							
8	00	Weekly Focus	Daily Detour	Daily Detour	Daily Detour	Daily Detour		
	30			Presentation		Presentation	Exercise	Read Book
9	00	Team Meeting			Report			Personal Time
	30	Buffer Time				Prep for Meeting		
10	00	Appointment						
	30							
11	00					Team Meeting		
	30							
12	00		Report					
	30							
1	00				Body Double			
	30				Avoided Tasks			
2	00							
	30							
3	00							
	30							
4	00							
	30							
5	00							
	30							
6	00	Dinner with Jordan	Exercise		Exercise			
	30							
7	00							
	30							

Figure 10.1   Intentional Planning.

about the chores and the long to-do list; give yourself permission to do the hobby, or relax. If you don't plan for it, it most likely won't happen; at least now, it stands a chance.

Urgent Tasks

These are tasks that made it to your priority list and are red tasks. Not every single red task needs to be scheduled. You may find some of these tasks happen independently, and your schedule is already built to give you time to work on them. It's helpful when you have a lot of obligations for the week and very little time. I will block time on the calendar to work, but I keep the tasks in the task manager and not on my calendar.

This is when intentional planning saves you stress and anxiety because you have a plan of when things will get done rather than wondering how you will make the deadline.

For example, during your Weekly Focus session, you see you have a report due on Friday morning. You have appointments all day on Monday and Wednesday. You don't know how long it will take to do the report, so you schedule the work session for Tuesday from 12 p.m. to 2 p.m. You schedule another time block for Thursday morning from 9 a.m. to 11 a.m. However, you know this may change depending on what happens on Tuesday; you will make any necessary adjustments after Tuesday's session.

Planning Tip

If you're wondering how you'll remember to check in with yourself after Tuesday's session and adjust the time block on Thursday, I have an answer. In your workbox, write a note of your plan wherever the breakdown is on your task manager or make a note on your calendar; better yet, set a reminder at the end of the session. The Weekly Focus and Daily Detours will also keep you on track. It feels like too much right now, but once you're in the new workflow, it won't feel like that.

Important Tasks

In the ADHD Priority Matrix, important tasks are green tasks. They are not due this week; they may not even have a due date. These tasks usually get passed by because there are more urgent things to do, but you would still like to do something with them before they turn into blaring, flashing red tasks.

These are tricky to time block only because the intention is a little different; timing is everything for this type of task. If you schedule it in the middle of your day, it won't get done. By now, you are already in your workday and will most likely not break this momentum to work on a green task.

It is recommended to schedule time blocks at the beginning of the day before you get into your busy daily work or after taking a lunch break. This gives you built-in transition time, a break before starting something new. It allows for a smoother transition between tasks and makes your workday more realistic. I recommend keeping the time blocks shorter, not exceeding an hour. This way, you can review the project, complete a couple of tasks, and then return to your daily work.

For example, you have a presentation due in two weeks, and it hasn't been started. It could wait until next week, but if you do that, it will make next week busy and stressful. It would be helpful if you could start this week. Now that you have some guidelines for planning intentionally, you decide the focus for this week is to have an outline of the presentation and a rough draft of the agenda. You schedule a time block for Wednesday and Friday (your least busy days) first thing in the morning after the Daily Detour. Each time block is for 30 minutes. On Friday, you will decide if you need to spend more time in the afternoon.

These kinds of time blocks make a huge difference in moving projects forward and prevent you from falling into an ADHD procrastination shame spiral. A time block of 30 minutes not only gets you started, but it boosts your confidence about the project, and makes you feel more in control of your time.

Workflow Tasks

In Chapter 7, we spent a lot of time talking about workflows. When you have a complete planning system, Planning Workflows are scheduled. Choose one day a week for the Weekly Focus and every day for a Daily Detour. Think about other areas in your work or personal life where a workflow could be scheduled. When they are done regularly on a certain day, it releases any stress of when something gets done; you have a plan, and now you can focus on what's important right now.

For example, you have blocked time from 10 to 10:30 a.m. every Friday to prep for the 11 a.m. team meeting. This gives you 30 minutes to prepare, leaving buffer time for distractions and transition time between the work and the meeting. This time block is scheduled weekly, so you don't have to worry about being unprepared, and it creates a nice structure for your schedule.

Transition Time

People with ADHD struggle with transitions and often do not account for them in their planning. It doesn't matter how big or little the transition is. Think about what it's like to return to work after a week of vacation; that first day back is often brutal. Then there is task switching, which happens during the day. It can be so hard to get started, and now you have to switch your focus; this is not an easy thing to do. When you schedule back-to-back meetings with no break in between, the likelihood of being late to more than one of those meetings is pretty high, let alone the mental stress of not feeling prepared and always feeling rushed. This is not a great way to spend your day.

Planning for transitions during the day is one of the best ways to support your ADHD.

It allows you to slow down, collect your thoughts, and capture whatever new information you need to process from the day. Take the time to document where you left off on a project, walk around, get some water, and clear your mind. Maybe do a breathing exercise or a short meditation before the next thing. Do what you need to do to get into the right mindset for what's next.

For example, you have a team meeting every Monday morning at 9 a.m., and your next appointment is at 10 a.m. You assume the team meeting will only last one hour. Sometimes this is true, but other times it's not, and you are late to the 10 a.m. meeting. Instead of scheduling the next meeting at 10 a.m., schedule it for 10:30. This adds buffer time if the meeting runs late and still gives you time to transition into something new with a calmer mindset.

Avoided Tasks

Avoided tasks are my favorite to intentionally plan for because we know that thinking you will do it tomorrow or next week doesn't get the task done. Avoided tasks can have many different reasons why they are being avoided; many times it's the emotion you feel about the task rather than the actual task itself. Let's be honest: setting a time to do it on your calendar doesn't really mean anything different than seeing it on your list. We need to treat these tasks a little bit differently.

1. **First, identify the roadblock.** It may be that the task is really a project and breaking it down into smaller and clearer steps is needed. It could be that you don't have all the information, so the task is not really a task yet. You think it's a tedious and boring task, and it keeps getting ignored. It's an email response that is late. You are embarrassed that it may be too late to send now and are not sure what to do.
2. **Second, deal with the roadblock.** Whatever the reason is, a decision needs to be made. Does the task stay on the list, get deleted, or get dated for future review? If it's staying on the list and is a priority to get it done, schedule a time block for it.
3. **Set up accountability.** Ask someone you trust to be your accountability partner. This can be a friend, family member, partner, spouse, boss, or co-worker. Let them know your plan and ask that they check in with you.
4. **Look for a body double.** You can ask your accountability partner or someone different, but working alongside someone else as you do the avoided task is like magic. It is so helpful to have the extra support and you can celebrate when it's done.

For example, regarding the unsent email, the longer it's avoided, the worse the feelings of shame and embarrassment become. Consider the facts: when was a response expected? If it's been three or more months, deleting the task may be best. If the person hasn't followed up, it may not be important. If it's been under three months, is the email still relevant? Do you want to know what you want to say? Do you know what they are expecting? If you decide it's worth responding, talk to your accountability partner and body double and set up an intentional time to write and send the email. Who knows, they may be able to help you write it. Then guess what—check that task off and move on.

What to Know About Time Blocking

Planning intentionally takes time to figure out, and it will look different depending on what it is you're protecting. The following are a few things that can turn up, and if you're aware of them, you will be able to plan for them and feel more confident about your planning.

Estimating How Long Tasks Take Is Not Required

It's true; the mission is not to complete the task but to work on it. Please read this again. The biggest reason people think they can't time block is because they don't know how long it will take them to do something. It's okay; you don't need to know. If you finish, great, but if you don't, that's okay; schedule another time block.

It Will Not Always Work; Please Don't Expect It To

Perfectionism will tell you that if the plan isn't perfect, it doesn't work. This is not true. It doesn't mean the strategy doesn't work; it means ADHD showed up and had a different plan. This is OK; it happens. Keep trying and practicing. Review the questions in the Coach's Corner to determine what's happening and course correct. You've got this.

Intentional Planning Is Flexible

This must be a flexible strategy because plans change all the time. It's OK to change your mind and decide to do something else. Priorities change, and what you thought was a good idea yesterday isn't a great idea today. It's OK if a meeting runs longer than expected; you start your time block 30 minutes later. It doesn't mean you have to drop it altogether. None of these things mean the strategy doesn't work; it simply means priorities changed.

It Works Best When Considering Energy Patterns

Schedule when you feel your best for avoided tasks and other difficult tasks. Have you ever noticed that you feel like you can conquer the world after you exercise? This happens because your brain releases dopamine, the feel-good feeling that helps with attention and clear thinking. The ADHD mind has less dopamine than a neurotypical brain and is always looking for ways to increase it. This is one of the reasons you're easily distracted during a boring conversation or not engaged in whatever you are doing.

When approaching an avoided task, I tell my clients they can be one of two kinds of people: Tigger or Eeyore from Winnie the Pooh. Tigger comes in full of energy and optimism, while Eeyore is an energy slump and is dragging his feet.

If you approach the task as Eeyore, you will likely continue to avoid it, find something else to do, and continue the cycle of pushing it into the future and feeling bad about it.

To find our inner Tigger and get the task done, look for your dopamine hits—the little things you like that increase your dopamine. For example, listen to your favorite music and have your own dance party. Play fetch with your dog for a couple of minutes. Do 10 jumping jacks and push-ups. The point is to get your heart rate up a little bit, so you feel can also conquer the world.

Let's be Tigger.

The Roadblocks of Planning Intentionally

As you practice intentional planning, you're building the flexibility muscle to react to changes during the day. The following are five common scenarios where planning intentionally doesn't work, with ideas on how to respond when they happen to you.

You Don't Want to Do It

This happens because what sounded like a great idea yesterday is not such a great idea today. Planning predicts the future; maybe you don't feel as motivated today as yesterday. When this happens, be aware of your internal conversation, and identify the limiting beliefs. For example, who says you can't change your mind? Replace judgment with curiosity. Ask the questions from the exercise above to better understand what's happening and consider other options to schedule the block of time differently. Consider a different time of day or shortening the interval you are blocking. Break the task down into even smaller action steps to help you get started with an early win.

You Are Avoiding the Task

This is different than not wanting to do it. Both scenarios are emotionally driven. Not wanting to do something may be because you don't have the energy, or you prefer to do something else. Avoiding the task is sneaky because you may not even realize it's happening because you are busy working on something during the time block, just not what you had planned.

Here are a few questions to consider if you're avoiding:

- What is it about the task that you are avoiding?
- What do you need to get started?
- When is the best time for you to work on these tasks?
- What length of time is best for you?
- How will you remember to do it?
- Who will you be accountable for?

Answering these questions gives you more information on how to better plan for this task. You are taking a proactive approach to getting it down in a way that supports your ADHD.

The Transition Didn't Happen

Let's say you have time blocked out from 2 to 3 p.m. to work on a project, but the meeting before took longer than you expected. You are going to be late for the time block. You have a decision to make. Do you still do what was planned, or do you adjust? This doesn't mean the time block failed; it means plans changed, and a decision will be made on what to do next. If this roadblock happens often, it's giving you good information for future planning. Consider starting and ending the meeting earlier to make your session or consider a later start time for the time block session. Somehow, the buffer time needs to be added to allow distractions and give you time to recenter and transition into the next task.

You Forgot About It

First, be kind and remember to practice self-compassion. This is ADHD showing up and distracting you from your original plan. It's going to happen but it's also not the end of the world, and you can adjust. Just like with the transition not happening, when you forget about a session, it's giving you information. Let's figure out why you forgot about it. Maybe you didn't open your workbox that day or didn't have a reminder set. If this is the case, set a reminder a few minutes before the time block to give you transition time.

It's No Longer a Priority

You already know it's OK to change your mind. Again, this is not saying planning intentionally doesn't work; it simply means priorities shifted, and you are consciously deciding to change the plan. If needed, reschedule the original time block to a different day or make notes to the workbox because you don't want to rely on your memory of why you made the switch.

When you approach roadblocks with curiosity rather than judgment, it opens opportunity.

Coaching Exercise

Let's take everything you've learned about intentional planning and see how it works best for you with the "Intentional Planning Exercise" (**Worksheet 14** in the appendix). If this is a new concept for you or you haven't had much success with it, let's start small. Follow these

200 UNAPOLOGETICALLY ADHD

instructions and then, at the end of the week, take some time to reflect on how it went:

1. **Choose one task. Pick something easy that you won't avoid.**
2. **Schedule a 30-minute time block.**
3. **Choose a realistic time to do the task.**
4. **Work with your ADHD. Review your personal data summary for guidance.**
5. **Set a reminder 10 minutes before the time block.**
6. **Track your progress for later reflection. Write down anything you notice, such as notes or ideas to remember later.**
7. **Write down what you notice. Include notes and ideas for later.**
8. **Repeat as often as you like.**
9. **At the end of the week, collect the data, and investigate.**
   - Did you do what you said you would do?
   - How did it feel to get it done? (Identify your benefits.)
   - How did you remember to do it?
   - How did the time framework feel—too long or too short?
   - Did you feel any resistance—from what?
   - If you didn't do it, what did you do instead?
   - Did you make that decision consciously?

This data provides excellent information on what's working and where it may need to be adjusted. Learning what doesn't work is just as valuable as learning what does work. For example, if you think four hours is too long a time period, shorten it to two hours. If you just need to start a project, consider a 10-minute block to open the email or file. You've started the project, which sometimes is the hardest thing to do. Adjust and tweak the time blocks as much as needed. The only rules for intentional planning are the ones you create.

Drafting Your Workflow Checklists

Review the chapter and add the action steps you want to include to your "Planning Workflow Builder" worksheet (Worksheet 13). The Weekly Focus session will spend more time in this step as you develop a rough draft for the upcoming week. Remember that this plan is subject to change and will most likely need to be adjusted. The Daily Detour is the time to make those adjustments and review the day ahead.

Planning Tip

To practice intentional planning, use the Intentional Planning Exercise worksheet (Worksheet 14 in the appendix). The exercise teaches you how to start with one small time block on your schedule. You can add more intentional planning to your week as you learn what works best for you.

Finalizing Your Workflow Checklists

Now that you've reviewed each step of the Planning Workflow (capture and collect, update and prioritize, and intentionally plan), it's time to decide what you want on your "Weekly Focus Checklist" worksheet (**Worksheet 15** in the appendix). Write down the steps to include in your custom checklists and any additional notes that are important to remember. The Weekly Focus checklist is more thorough and takes around 30–45 minutes. Figure 10.2 shows an example of the Weekly Focus Checklist.

Now do the same thing with the "Daily Detour Checklist" worksheet (**Worksheet 16** in the appendix). The Daily Detour takes around 10–15 minutes daily to focus on the calendar and time blocks and adjust your daily priorities. Figure 10.3 shows an example of the Daily Detour Checklist.

Final Thoughts About the Weekly Focus and Daily Detour Checklists

These checklists are set up to accommodate your ADHD. Working memory is an executive function that is often challenged with ADHD. You can look at your calendar and see you have an appointment in 10 minutes and then get distracted by a colleague and forget about your appointment until later in the day.

Workflows take time to become a habit, and you risk forgetting steps if you don't have the checklist in front of you. It will keep you focused, and you will know where you left off if you do get distracted.

Continue to practice your Planning Workflows and make adjustments when needed. Remember a good enough plan is better than a perfect plan that never happens.

Weekly Focus

Complete the steps of the Weekly Focus Checklist. This should take no longer than 30–45 minutes.

- ☐ Gather planning tools and supplies
- ☐ Turn off notifications
- ☐ Breathing exercise
- ☐ Reflection - Set timer for 5 minutes
- ☐ Collect new information from inboxes
- ☐ Update workbox with new information
- ☐ Review workbox for any needed adjustments
- ☐ Prioritize tasks for the week
- ☐ Decide on which tasks to intentionally plan
- ☐ Schedule time blocks with reminders

Notes:

Check inboxes: text messages, email, and notebook. Review meeting notes for potential tasks. Cross-check work and home calendar to make sure nothing is overbooked.

Figure 10.2　Weekly Focus Checklist sample.

Daily Detour

Complete the steps of the Daily Detour Checklist. This
should take no longer than 10 minutes.

- [ ] Check inboxes for new information
- [ ] Review calendar for today's appointments
- [ ] Update appointments if needed
- [ ] Review task manager
- [ ] Update or adjust tasks where needed
- [ ] Review time blocks
- [ ] Adjust time blocks as needed
- [ ] _____
- [ ] _____

Notes:

Check inboxes: text messages, email, and notebook. Prepare

for today's appointments. Cross-check work and home

calendars to make sure nothing is overbooked.

Figure 10.3   Daily Detour Checklist sample.

Coach's Corner

There will always be things to do, and putting ourselves first on the
calendar is difficult. You say no to the things you wished you had time for
and yes to things out of guilt. Life has too many *shoulds*. There are always
things to do, and yes, we need to figure out how to do them, but not at
the expense of the things that bring you joy and make you feel alive.

Planning intentionally goes beyond the scheduled time block on
your calendar. It allows you to design your life. Have you heard this
term before? What does it mean to you? For me, it goes back to my

intention, what is the reason I'm doing this? What do I hope to experience? What do I want in life? Where am I right now in achieving it? What am I missing? What am I so grateful for? What do I want to do more or less of? How do I make these thoughts come true?

So many questions, but this is the kind of reflection that is necessary if it's time for you to make changes in your life. If you're unhappy with your job, look for a new one that brings you purpose. I know this is not easy, but it is possible; I witness it all the time. Is there an aspect of your life that is lacking? Last year, I was missing time for my spiritual life. My best friend and I went to a wellness retreat for five days, and it brought me back to my inner peace. It was transformational and a reminder that we must be intentional with our time to make these experiences happen. Are you in relationships where you're always apologizing? Maybe it's time to evaluate who deserves your time and attention.

But guess what? It's not just these big areas of life that need attention; it's the small things that can change today. Are you saying yes to things that you don't have time for? It's OK to say, "Thank you for thinking of me, but it's not going to work." And don't apologize. You do not need to say you're sorry for protecting your time. You do not need to explain why you said no. You do not need to sacrifice your well-being for someone else. Intentionally put space in your calendar to breathe, slow down, and care for yourself. You are worth it.

Chapter Summary

The following are the key points from the chapter:

- Intentional planning is where the calendar meets your to-do list.
- It protects your time to do what you need and want to do.
- It's not just for productive tasks—also plan for fun, connection, and joy.
- It puts glasses on time blindness (ADHD support for the win).
- Hyper-scheduling and time blocking are not the same thing.
- There's more to life than just your to-do list—go have some fun.

Congratulations! You've almost completed the journey. We've covered the importance of supporting your ADHD and why planning is more complicated than one might think. You created a workbox with planning tools that support you and your ADHD. You created workflow checklists that are specific to your Weekly Focus and Daily Detour sessions.

You, my friend, have a complete planning system that is resilient and flexible for change.

In the final chapter, we discuss what happens next, what you can expect, and how to keep your system resilient and flexible to change.

11

Planning for the Future

You DID IT! You are well on your way to confidently taking control of your time. However, you may still be afraid that this will not last or that you will end up in the same place you were before reading this book.

I can't say for sure, but I will say this. If you followed the steps in choosing the tools for your workbox, clarified your workflow, and adjusted your weekly focus and daily detours to work for you, I'm willing to bet things will be different the next time you find yourself wondering if you need a new task manager or are feeling overwhelmed by the disorganization of your projects and tasks.

In this last chapter, we focus on preparing for the future. It guides you on what to do when your systems break and how to recover. We also cover connecting your long-term projects and goals to your weekly planning.

Systems Are Essential with ADHD

When you have ADHD, it's crucial to establish structures and systems to address challenges with time management, planning, organization, and productivity. You, my friend, have these systems. Following this book's framework, you've created a customized planning system that supports you and your ADHD. The framework taught is flexible, and there is always an opportunity to make the necessary adjustments to make the system function for you.

The planning system is resilient even on the days and weeks when your ADHD is the loudest.

Your planning system and ADHD are friends, and you are friends with the planning system and your ADHD. These systems are no longer to be feared; they are welcomed because they make your life easier.

If it's been a while since you've talked, that's OK. Spend some time to catch up—visit and say hello. It's not going to be mad, and it's not going to judge you. If you forget what to do, pick up this book and review the process again. This is expected; we are not supporting your ADHD if we think any differently, and this is not a limiting belief or taking on a pessimistic attitude. This is what radically accepting ADHD looks like (Chapter 1). You will have great days, and there will be days when you throw your hands up in the air, go to sleep, and start over tomorrow. When you embrace the reality of this happening, you can stop apologizing for it or wonder what you are doing wrong. This is part of your ADHD, and leaning into it will serve you much better than trying to fight it every day.

It Takes Practice

How many professional athletes practice their sport for a couple of weeks, maybe a month or so, and become the best they can be? Silly question, right? No one practices something for a month and then becomes the very best of their sport, just like buying the best hammer will not instantly make me a carpenter.

Practicing it is the only way to know if your planning system works.

Be aware of any perfectionist tendencies that may show up, because these will keep you from using the system. Don't waste time wondering if you named a project correctly or if you should have a label or a tag. Experiment and be curious about what you find out.

There are no rules to break or right or wrong ways to organize projects. Your planning systems are not static and are meant to change as your needs change.

Don't be afraid to set up a project incorrectly or to make mistakes.

This is often when the real learning shows up. Instead of assuming that you did something wrong or that the system does not work, be curious.

Review When It's Not Working

It's true that the best lessons sometimes come not from succeeding but from failing. Not only does it tell us what's working and what's not, but there is also a lot to learn about how we respond to failure. It hurts, but to radically accept who we are, we must somehow find a way to move on from that initial gut punch and use this new knowledge to continue living the life we were meant to live. This is our responsibility and no one else's.

If you don't take control of your schedule, someone else will.

Our lives are governed by time, a finite resource with an unknown quantity. When we make plans, we are essentially trying to predict the future, but since none of us are psychic, we do our best with what we have. This gives us some sense of control over our lives. However, even the most meticulously planned events, with the best intentions, do not guarantee success.

Because of this reality, it's important to learn how to be flexible and resilient with our plans. When the unexpected happens, and your workbox becomes less trustworthy, it's time to figure out what is getting in your way.

Watch for the Warning Signs

Systems do not fall apart overnight; it happens over some time. It's important to recognize the warning signs. The smaller the time gap, the easier it will be to get it back up and running smoothly.

Here is what you want to be paying attention to:

- It's been over a week since you've looked at your workbox.
- You are no longer doing daily detours.
- The last weekly focus was over two weeks ago, and not because you were on vacation.
- You're using more supporting tools to keep organized rather than the two most important, the calendar and task manager.
- You no longer trust that the workbox has the most current information.

What's Going On?

You've noticed there is a problem, but now what? We must figure out what's happening and then look for solutions to get back on track. Start with the two main tools in the workbox, the calendar and task manager.

Ask the following questions:

- What's keeping you from reviewing the workbox? Is this something that's within your control? What adjustments do you need to make to pay attention to it again?
- How are your reminders working? Are they set at the right time? Are you noticing them?
- What are you doing instead of looking at your workbox? Is this a conscious decision? How are you capturing new information like meetings and new tasks right now?
- What are you most afraid of about returning to your workbox? Is it the number of overdue tasks? The avoidance of having to take the time to update it? Are you afraid you've forgotten something important?
- What are you missing when the workbox is out of date? How are you feeling now compared to when the workbox was working? What areas in your life do you need to pay attention to, to get caught back up? (Start with one; trying to catch on to everything will only add to the overwhelm.)

When you reflect on what's getting in your way, you will notice the answers to how to get it back to working have been inside you the whole time.

Before, it was easy to assume it was the tool or you, but now you know differently. You have the agency to get it back and running in no time.

Time to Get Back to Work

You've identified where the friction is happening; now it's time to take action and get your workbox working again.

Here are the steps to get started:

1. Schedule time in your calendar to update your tools. This is another great example of where intentional planning works. You will need to experiment with the amount of time for each session and how many you are willing to do weekly or daily.
2. Gather any new appointments, projects, or tasks from your inboxes.
3. Review the calendar first; this will most likely require the least updating. Add any new appointments and double-check that there isn't any overbooking. Update any appointments that have been canceled or postponed.
4. First, review the "Today" view for digital task manager systems. Go through the list and check off any tasks that are no longer relevant or have been completed.
5. Review your past-due tasks and update the dates. (In Chapter 9, review the difference between a due date and a review date.)
6. Review your areas and projects and update any necessary tasks.
7. If you use a paper planner combined with your digital task manager, begin with the calendar and update it with the most current information.
8. Review your task lists and rewrite a list with the most current projects and tasks if needed.
9. If seeing the empty pages from the past bothers you, tear them out. There's no reason to feel bad about what did or didn't happen in the past. Your mission is only to look ahead.
10. Update anything else in your paper planner that you feel is necessary.

Start Again

It's normal to feel some anxiety returning to your workbox. All kinds of emotions will show up. The one I see most often is shame and disappointment around letting it go in the first place. Clients have told me that it helps to journal what they were doing at the time and see on paper what was taking up space in their lives. This is the time to practice the same self-compassion you would offer to someone else. Please remember, you built this to be resilient because you are resilient.

Updating and changing priorities is not something to run away from; it's something to embrace because it's part of living on your own terms.

Once the workbox is updated, you can start again as if no time has passed. You worked hard to build this system, and it's not as fragile as you once thought. You can take control of the situation and get back to feeling confident in your planning.

This Is ADHD

Hiya, Jordan. This has been quite a ride. If you've been keeping up with the book chapter by chapter, creating your new systems and muscling your way through it all, I'll bet dollars to donuts that you're exhausted right about now.

This is ADHD.

Let's take a breath or two and embrace that exhaustion. Planning with ADHD is a high-calorie burn activity. You think typing a few calendar entries into your planner or marking up a page in a notebook should be easy because you've been told all your life that it's easy. It's not easy. It's never been easy. The dirty truth is that it will never be easy.

So breathe it in. Hold on to it. Recognize that what you're doing is hard. Because once you let that breath out, it'll be time to move forward again.

This is ADHD.

I was diagnosed with ADHD 25 years ago. I've spent those 25 years trying to figure out two things: what in the hey-hoo took so long for me to get the diagnosis in the first place, and how do I keep moving forward in my life from that point? Whether you're new to your diagnosis or you've been living with ADHD since you were a kiddo, you might just know a thing or two about those feelings.

So maybe you've lived with ADHD for a while. You survived the dark and anxious years. You soared through the introspective we-must-learn-everything years. You somehow hung on through the did-I-lose-all-my-friends years. Maybe you lost some jobs. You probably quit some jobs. Did you ever run away from some jobs?

It's way too easy to reminisce about the challenging times while staring joy square in the face. In spite of all those hard times, ADHD has also illuminated the dark corners of uncertainty in my own life. It has allowed me to unlock pieces of myself I didn't know existed. I am amazed to this very day when I learn something about myself that serves to rewrite my story in some way. Thanks to ADHD, I'm learning new things about myself all the time.

How does all this apply to the systems we use to plan? Outstanding segue, Jordan.

I believe that people living with ADHD who commit to developing resilient systems that allow them to live the lives they want to live are people of utmost courage. These are people who have conquered the fear of trying, who have discovered the desire to connect to a world beyond themselves and engage with it. They are people who understand that they will sometimes break the promises they make to themselves and others because their brains are fascinating and unpredictable. In spite of this unpredictability, they stand up, return to their systems, and try again. Courageous people know they are not perfect, and even so they are willing to keep trying.

Last words on this subject, I promise, then I'll move along. But it's important, and I hope you've picked up on it on every page leading up to this one in this book. You're going to put a lot of time into building systems that you believe will work for you, and they're going to fall to pieces. But that's OK. It's OK because you're still here. You're alive and breathing. You're an agent of action and learning and creativity and you'll be ready to try something new tomorrow.

This is ADHD.

Connecting Long-Term Planning to Your Week

One of the biggest obstacles with ADHD is the difficulty of planning for the future. ADHD minds tend to be anchored in the present moment; if it's not happening now, it's not happening. The future feels abstract and far away, making planning difficult. Many factors are at play here, including the number of executive functions (Chapter 1) that are required to plan. If a new project or an event you must plan for comes in, it's difficult to break these down into smaller action steps without getting too far into the details or not having enough details. Time blindness shows up because it's difficult to estimate how long things will take, so how do you plan with any kind of accuracy?

Many people get stuck in procrastination (yes, another P word) when they wait too long to get started and then rush to the finish line. This doesn't feel great because you overwork yourself and feel horrible for not starting sooner.

Is there an ADHD-friendly way to connect long-term planning to your weekly schedule?

Yes, there is, but we must keep things simple. Otherwise, if it's too complicated, you risk avoiding it *again*. You may be wondering if adding this to your to-do list is worthwhile or if it will just add more stress.

The Benefits of Long-Term Planning

The benefits of long-term planning will be different for everyone. Some might find that having a plan in place feels good and that it's worth the extra time to look into the future and break down the project into some kind of daily or weekly task. Others might find it helpful, but only to a degree; they want to be reminded of upcoming projects but do not care to break them down until they come closer.

Here are a few key benefits to long-term planning:

- **Provides direction:** Identifying what we want—from big career changes to daily habits like exercise and looking ahead—reminds us of upcoming special events and projects coming.
- **Enables prioritization:** Having many goals in life is common, but time is limited. Prioritize what's important now and accept that not everything can be done at once.
- **Encourages progress:** If we see something coming up in the future and start to plan for it now, we can keep track of our progress by checking in with ourselves monthly and weekly.
- **Allows for adjustments:** The check-ins allow us to adjust as needed and maybe even change our minds. It gives our flexibility muscle practice without judgment.

- **Helps with time blindness:** When there are concrete deadlines to our projects, having a planned time to check in helps you see the future and how close you are to reaching the deadline. It closes the gap between Now and Not Now—you are checking in on your progress and assessing what's next.

The most important factor is what is most important to you and what you need. Anything we suggest here is only a framework and can be adjusted.

What's Wrong with Goal Setting?

In Chapter 7, I mentioned a client who would rather have a root canal than set goals. One of the reasons for this is that it was a constant reminder of what he wasn't doing. In my own experience, I've had the same New Year's resolutions for the last 20 years. I finally gave up on the idea because it wasn't motivating me to take action. Don't get me wrong—I think it's great to focus on different aspects of ourselves and what we want in life, but there must be a better way than the traditional goal-setting exercises we've been taught.

I was leading an accountability coaching group, and at first we set the group for everyone to share their goal for the week, and then the next week they would update how it was going. Many members of the group reported that they didn't meet the goal. Digging into this a bit further, I found out that many believed success meant the goal must be obtained and completed.

With this definition, you can imagine why so many people felt like they were failing. Let's say your goal was to work out three times this week, but you could only work out two times. Failed! You didn't meet the goal. Here's another example: your goal is to start working on an upcoming work project, but when you sit down to work on it, you are overwhelmed because you don't know where to start. Failed! You didn't meet the goal of getting started (which is a vague goal, anyway).

What was supposed to be a positive coaching experience turned into something entirely different. After some discussion, we decided to change direction, and instead of a goal, we chose our focus for the week. It already sounds nicer, doesn't it?

Your focus doesn't measure if you completed something; it measures your effort and is recognized as a continued work in progress.

If the focus was to exercise three times this week, and you did it two times, this is something to acknowledge and celebrate. It's not something to feel bad about. If you felt overwhelmed with starting a project, let's celebrate that you tried and focus on how to help you find the starting point.

In terms of long-term planning, we are looking at two different things:

1. Choose an area in your life to focus on.
2. Identify upcoming events and projects that you want to prepare for.

Where to Start

In Chapter 4, we discussed the "Internal Compass" and "Wheel of Life" exercises (Worksheets 2 and 5). If you have not completed them or it's been a while since you did, please do these two exercises to clarify your values and understand what areas of your life you would like to spend more time on. You do not need to complete these exercises every time you plan long-term. As long as they are updated and you can review them later, you're good to go.

Please use the "Long-Term Planning" worksheet (**Worksheet 17** in the appendix) to follow along as I explain the process that takes you to review three months at a time—a quarterly review. If you want to reflect on where you want to be 5 or 10 years from now, great; go for it. What I have found is that thinking too far ahead in the future can cause a lot of stress and anxiety. I like to start small; you can build from here if you want to go further.

Choose an Area in Your Life to Focus On

The Wheel of Life is a great resource for deciding what area of life you want to focus on for the next three months.

Here is a summary of what each area means and examples of potential places of focus:

- **Personal:** Pursue a new hobby or make time to work on a current one, such as scheduling more time for rest and self-care.
- **Health:** Improve physical health with exercise, such as adopting a healthier diet or eating habits.
- **Home:** Work on things like decluttering the home, or a remodeling or gardening project.
- **Relationships:** Focus on staying in touch with loved ones and meeting new people.
- **Recreation:** Bring more joy into your life by scheduling time for activities you love.
- **Spirituality:** Reconnect with your faith, such as by implementing a meditation practice.
- **Career:** Implement a new job search, increase a specific skill with training, or start a business.
- **Finance:** Create a budget, save for a large purchase, or set up a retirement fund.

It's normal to feel that *all* areas of your life need attention. Some of these ideas may resonate with you, and you feel the urgency of implementing everything right now. But you also know there is limited time, and if you've ever tried to do too many things at once, you know it doesn't turn out that great.

Imagine the impact you can make when you focus on one area and see results, instead of trying to work on too many things and then abandoning everything.

Here is a step-by-step process for getting your priorities clear (Use the Long-Term Planning worksheet [Worksheet 17 in the appendix] to write down your information):

1. Review your ratings and write them on the worksheet. Identify the areas with the lowest rating. Consider which ones would have the biggest impact if you are paying attention to them.
2. Take the two areas with the lowest numbers, brainstorm, and write your ideas and projects for each area.
3. Use the Long-Term Planning Priority Matrix (Figure 11.1) to decide which of the two areas to focus on for the next three months. In this version of the Priority Matrix, we are focused on real deadlines and high-impact projects.

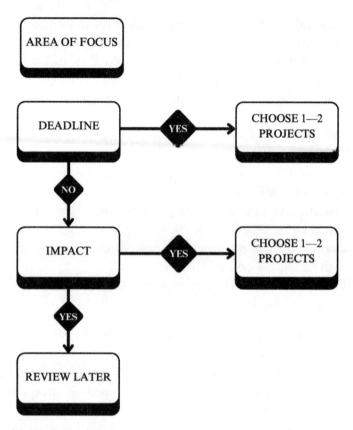

Figure 11.1   Priority Matrix.

In addition to using the Priority Matrix as a guide, here are a few additional questions to consider:

- How many areas of focus connect to your values?
- Do you have the capacity and time to take on something new right now?
- What areas of focus will make you feel more energized and motivated?
- How much effort will it take to succeed?
- Which focus areas will lay a foundation for other future areas of focus?
- Where can you find some easy wins to build momentum?

Now that you know your focus area, you can break it down into smaller steps and decide how to incorporate it into your weekly plan.

Before we get to that, we need to review upcoming events and projects in the next three months.

Preview What's Coming Ahead

Setting our focus aside, let's look ahead to upcoming events and projects. For long-term planning, I love having a yearly calendar that shows all 12 months, separated by each quarter, to capture a real visual of time passing (Figure 11.2). This is very difficult to do on your phone or even looking at only 1 month at a time.

YEARLY EVENTS		
JANUARY	FEBRUARY	MARCH
APRIL	MAY	JUNE
JULY	AUGUST	SEPTEMBER
OCTOBER	NOVEMBER	DECEMBER

Figure 11.2   Yearly Events.

The process I will walk you through is like the Weekly Focus Workflow:

1. Review your inboxes for upcoming events, meetings, or appointments and add to the calendar.
2. If necessary, add new projects to your task manager.
3. If necessary, update current projects to your task manager.
4. Break down any projects where you need more clarity on the next steps.
5. Add the dates, tags, and other details in your task manager.

Planning Tip

Consider using a mind map to brainstorm the milestones and actions required. This is an excellent tool for nonlinear thinkers because it allows you to get your thoughts out of your head as they come and the flexibility to move things around as needed.

In summary, you have your chosen focus area, and your workbox is updated with upcoming events and projects.

Half of your long-term planning is done!

There isn't anything else you need to do with the upcoming events and new projects. You did the work of looking ahead and entering the most important information in your workbox. As the next three months pass, these new events will show up as you planned for them to do.

What's next is incorporating these new events into your weekly schedule.

Connecting Your Focus

First, we will review your chosen focus area. Use the "Long-Term Planning" worksheet (**Worksheet 17** in the appendix) to list the projects and action steps you wish to accomplish in the next 30, 60, and 90 days. This exercise is not about perfection and is supposed to focus on broader ideas; we are not at the point where specifics and clarity are needed. We have to work our way toward clarity. Write down what comes to mind, and if you need help, find someone you trust to help you break it down.

Figure 11.3 provides an example of how this might look if your focus area is to implement an exercise routine.

Quarterly Plan

List the milestones and actions for 30 days, 60 days, and 90 days for each area of focus.

Area of Focus   Exercise

90 DAYS

Walk for 30 minutes, 3 times per week.

60 DAYS

Include one 5-minute activity daily.

30 DAYS

Track my walks/activities to build accountability.

Figure 11.3   Quarterly Plan.

Next, we want to take the monthly ideas and break them down into weekly tasks (Figure 11.4).

Finally, review the weekly tasks and identify which ones you want to do daily (for example, 15 minutes of active movement every day). See Figure 11.5.

Take Action

Break down the milestones and actions steps weekly for each area of focus.

Area of Focus _____Exercise_____

WEEK ONE

Go for a 10-minute walk 2 times.
Do a 2-minute yoga/ stretch daily.

WEEK TWO

Increase walks to 15 minutes, 3 times.
Yoga/ stretch daily plus add 5 squats.

WEEK THREE

Increase walks to 20 minutes, 3 times.
Yoga/ stretch daily plus add 10 squats and 5 pushups.

WEEK FOUR

Increase walks to 30 minutes, 3 times.
Yoga/ stretch daily plus 15 bodyweight exercises daily.

Figure 11.4   Take Action.

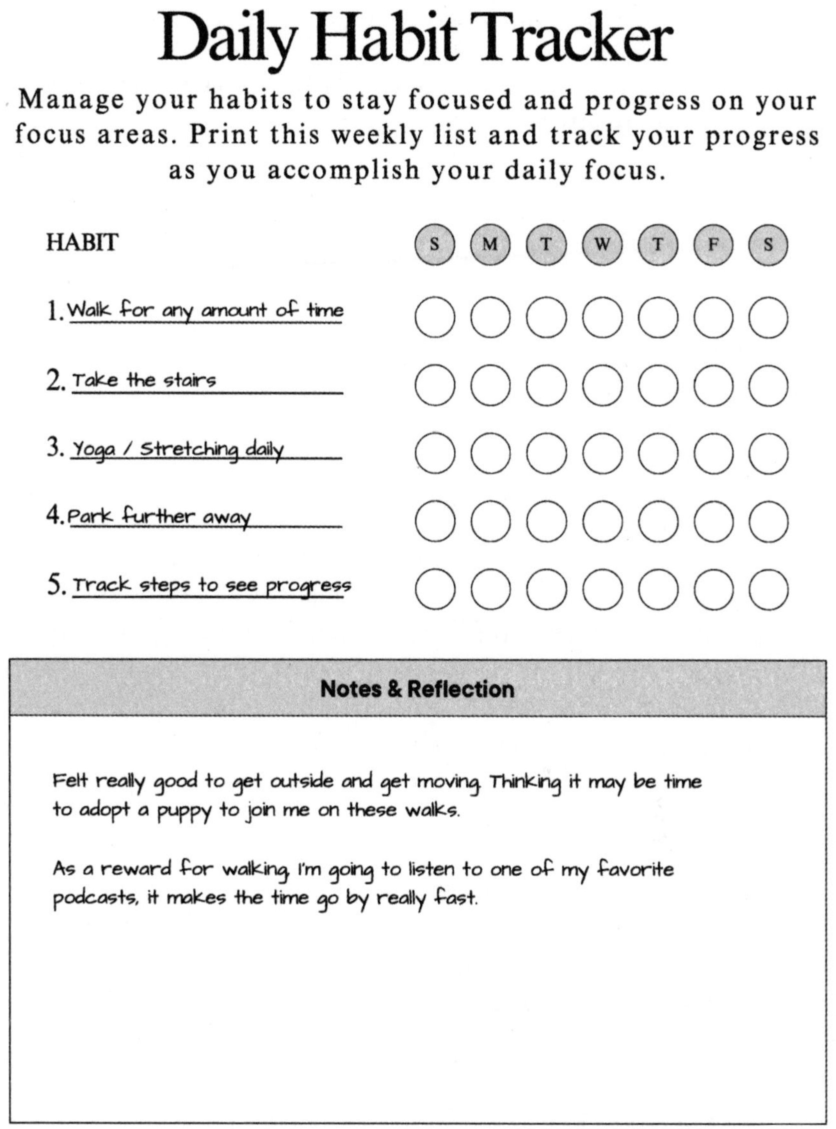

Daily Habit Tracker

Manage your habits to stay focused and progress on your focus areas. Print this weekly list and track your progress as you accomplish your daily focus.

HABIT   (S) (M) (T) (W) (T) (F) (S)

1. Walk for any amount of time   ○ ○ ○ ○ ○ ○ ○

2. Take the stairs   ○ ○ ○ ○ ○ ○ ○

3. Yoga / Stretching daily   ○ ○ ○ ○ ○ ○ ○

4. Park further away   ○ ○ ○ ○ ○ ○ ○

5. Track steps to see progress   ○ ○ ○ ○ ○ ○ ○

Notes & Reflection

Felt really good to get outside and get moving. Thinking it may be time to adopt a puppy to join me on these walks.

As a reward for walking, I'm going to listen to one of my favorite podcasts, it makes the time go by really fast.

Figure 11.5   Daily Habit Tracker.

Designing a Workflow

Just as you designed a workflow for your weekly and daily detour sessions, you may benefit from designing a workflow around your focus area. This keeps it as a main focus for the week, and there is less chance of you forgetting about it.

Here are a few ideas on how to do this:

- Add to your Weekly Focus and Daily Detour checklists to check in on your quarterly focus.
- Intentionally plan a weekly reoccurring appointment to work on the focus.
- Schedule the time when you feel focused, energized, and at your best.
- Practice the time intervals until you find something that works most of the time.
- Find an accountability partner who may be working on something themselves. Support each other by setting up a regular time to check in.
- Celebrate and acknowledge your progress each week.

This concludes the discussion of connecting your long-term planning to your weekly schedule. It takes some time to find a streamlined workflow that works best for you. I advise keeping it simple and focusing only on one new area at a time. This framework isn't different from what you've already learned in the book, and you need to practice, evaluate, and adjust when needed.

Coach's Corner

This chapter covers two major themes: how to bounce back from a broken planning system and how to incorporate long-term planning into your weekly planning. They both have in common that you are preparing for the future. The reality is that your planning system will need attention at some point, and new events and projects will always be on the horizon.

What's different now is that you have the resources and agency to recover from the broken system and to plan ahead more confidently by following a process similar to the one you follow during the Weekly Focus sessions. If you ever doubt yourself, remember you are resilient and will continue to persevere like you always have. I hope this time it will be with fewer apologies and more living life on your own terms.

Chapter Summary

The following are the key points from the chapter:

- Practice is the only way to know what works and doesn't.
- Don't let perfection get in your way. Embrace the mistakes as learning opportunities.
- Pay attention to the red flags when friction appears in your planning system.
- Take action to get your tools updated and back to running together.
- Success isn't only about completion. Include the effort and the work that is being done toward completion.
- Start with one focus area to plan for the next three months.
- Review and update the workbox with new information in the next three months.
- Design a workflow around your chosen area of focus to include it in your weekly plan.

Congratulations! You have reached the end of the book. It has been a journey to take such a deep dive into planning. We've covered the importance of supporting your ADHD and why planning is more complicated than one might think. You created a workbox with planning tools that support you and your ADHD, with workflow checklists specific to your Weekly Focus and Daily Detour sessions. The book ends with resources on what to do if friction happens in your system and how to incorporate long-term planning into the weekly plan.

You, my friend, have a complete planning system that is resilient and flexible to change. It wasn't easy to get here. We hope this book will be a reference for you anytime you need a refresher. Thank you so much for your time and attention. We invite you to read our final thoughts.

Conclusion

PETE AND I presented at the international ADHD conference, on the topic *How to Create Joy in Your Life When You Are Spiraling with ADHD*. Unfortunately, what stops more people from feeling joy in their lives is the shame they feel. One of the missions of our presentation was to help decrease the recovery time it takes from being in an ADHD shame spiral to finding calm and joy in your life. The good news is you don't have to look far to find it.

It's important to understand that joy and happiness are different. Although they are both emotions, happiness measures how good you feel over time, while joy measures the body's experience at any given moment.

Here are a few examples:

- Your pets greeting you at the front door
- The first sip of coffee in the morning
- Your favorite music
- Watching a funny video, TV, or movie
- Connecting with a dear friend
- Hearing your children laugh
- Trying something new
- Working on a hobby
- Anything that puts a smile on your face

What if these things, these little moments of joy, were also included on your to-do list? How would it change your life? How would it change others around you? Joy is contagious. When you slow down to notice, others notice you slowing down, and it permits them to do it too.

Take a moment, right now, to close your eyes and take a long, deep breath in and exhale. You are living, my friend—now do it unapologetically.

Failure

Where did you learn your views on failure? Years past, I think I might have answered that I learned mine from my parents. They had reasonably high expectations of me as a student, particularly in high school. They pushed me to pursue my interests with intention and enthusiasm. But as I sit here writing this essay, I can't for the life of me remember a situation in which my parents came down on me for failing at something.

I went to a competitive high school with kids who, if I'm completely honest, had a much higher degree of interest in the raw work of academics than I did. I don't know if they failed often. I only noticed them when I failed.

I'm not talking about traditional letter-grade failure, mind you. Sure, there was that. Remember, I was diagnosed with ADHD as an adult. In high school, my ADHD was an undiagnosed playboy. The roller coaster of grade performance was a natural outcome of having no idea who I really was as a human being.

The sort of failure I'm talking about is the tiny, paper-cut failure. This is the kind of failure that reinforces the image you hold of yourself as less than, as someone who can't keep up with peers. This is the picture of the imposter.

I built up my understanding of success through a reflection of my shortcomings in others' successes. I used that reflection as a blunt instrument with which to beat myself in the form of disastrously negative self-talk and limiting beliefs that only served to reinforce success as something I was progressively farther from reaching.

Where did I learn my views on failure? I learned it all from myself. I created my own perception that failure is something to be feared and avoided at all costs. It carried with it the emotional weight of shame, disappointment, anxiety, and doubt. I was a kid. Why would I want to explore anything in the orbit of those planets thoughtfully?

But failure only carries that weight because we have allowed it to. Absent our relationship with it, failure is just a state of change, a signal to redirect energy in a new, more effective direction.

Look to the scientists in your life, Jordan, because they get it. A failure reveals an opportunity to improve or refine a hypothesis before testing that hypothesis again. A failure is a single step on a longer journey toward expanding knowledge. A failure helps us to refine the questions we ask of ourselves and the world around us. A failure condition is an objective fact, free of judgment and emotional weight, if you are able to approach it as such. Most important, failure is not an end. It is the beginning of another opportunity for change.

ADHD taught me to judge myself through the lens of failure when I was a child, no one else. I've been working much of my adult life to reframe that childish interpretation of failure and take ownership of the word for what it is: a powerful token for observing transformation. If I stop judging failure so harshly, I experience less anxiety over my imperfections. If failure is an opportunity for growth, I am more resilient when I'm faced with obstacles. If failure is a data point and nothing more, I maintain a healthier view of my own self-worth.

ADHD can be a harsh and persistent partner. At the very same time, it can be the key to unlocking connections and patterns in the world that remain hidden to so many. ADHD is a

(continued)

(*continued*)

bounteous vessel of creativity and joy. If we are to assign weight to any emotional connection to ADHD, let that weight fall on exhilaration, cleverness, grit, and determination.

Listen for failure's wisdom when your efforts go astray.

Mine the riches from each fallen effort. Let curious questions flow, and promising new directions emerge from the ashes of plans laid low.

Failures are simply signposts on the road of wonder.

You are not measured by a single attempt but by the determination you carry to learn and grow. Who can stop this unbending reed? The root grows deeper with each passing storm.

So steel yourselves. The path stretches before us, and failure travels with us, not to shame or slow our stride but to illuminate the way forward. We will greet it as a teacher, an old friend.

And we will succeed, not by avoiding failure, but by embracing the power it gives us to evolve.

Onward now. There is much to be done. We shall do it with courage.

Thank you for allowing us to walk this journey with you. It began with learning how ADHD impacts the way you see planning and time. You answered several questions in each chapter to better understand who you are. Answering these questions is difficult, and it takes courage to open yourself up to beliefs and thoughts you don't want to see. It's uncomfortable, but it also comes along with fundamental transformation.

What happens if (*fill in the blank*)? It changes your story. Your journey with time doesn't stop with implementing these ideas into your life. There will be good days and bad days. We hope you remember to be grateful for the good days, and give yourself the same grace you offer to a loved one on the bad days.

You are resilient. You are worthy. And you are *unapologetically* ADHD.

Appendix: Planning Worksheets

THIS APPENDIX CONTAINS the worksheets in the book. You can copy and print them or fill them out in the book.

This table shows where the worksheets are referenced in the book.

Worksheet 1: Intentions Exercise

Intentions Exercise

This exercise will guide you in creating a mission statement for this book. Answer the three questions below with 2–3 words and combine them to form a mission statement of 1–2 sentences.

Questions

1. What do you want?

_____

2. Why do you want it?

_____

3. How will you get it?

_____

Mission Statement:

_____

_____

_____

_____

_____

Worksheet 2: Your Internal Compass

Your Internal Compass

Choose all the traits you relate to that build your personal set of beliefs.

☐ Accountability	☐ Freedom	☐ Perseverance
☐ Adventure	☐ Friendship	☐ Quality
☐ Ambition	☐ Fun	☐ Reliability
☐ Authenticity	☐ Generosity	☐ Resilience
☐ Balance	☐ Gratitude	☐ Respect
☐ Cooperation	☐ Health	☐ Responsibility
☐ Compassion	☐ Honesty	☐ Self-acceptance
☐ Community	☐ Honor	☐ Self-awareness
☐ Courage	☐ Humility	☐ Self-confidence
☐ Creativity	☐ Inclusivity	☐ Self-discipline
☐ Curiosity	☐ Independence	☐ Simplicity
☐ Determination	☐ Integrity	☐ Sincerity
☐ Diversity	☐ Kindness	☐ Spirituality
☐ Education	☐ Knowledge	☐ Sustainability
☐ Environmentalism	☐ Learning	☐ Teamwork
☐ Equality	☐ Love	☐ Tolerance
☐ Exploration	☐ Loyalty	☐ Trustworthiness
☐ Fairness	☐ Open-mindedness	☐ Unity
☐ Family	☐ Originality	☐ Understanding
☐ Flexibility	☐ Patience	☐ Well-being
☐ Forgiveness	☐ Peace	☐ Wisdom

Worksheet 3: Personal Data Summary

Personal Data Summary

This worksheet highlights the most important information you should remember while creating your system. It will also remind you of your preferences and how ADHD affects your life. You can add any additional information you think is important but was not included in the exercises or assessments.

Your Mission Statement

_____

_____

Top 5 Values

1. _____
2. _____
3. _____
4. _____
5. _____

Top 5 Strengths

1. _____
2. _____
3. _____
4. _____
5. _____

Worksheet 4: Finding Your Strengths

Finding Your Strengths

There are many advantages to understanding your strengths. It increases happiness and well-being, boosts relationships, and helps manage stress and anxiety. Review some of the options below to learn more about your strengths and how to use them daily.

VIA Character Strengths Survey

The VIA Character Strengths Survey is a 10-minute, online questionnaire used to determine your top strengths and where you excel the most.

The basic survey is offered for free on the VIA Institute of Character website: www.viacharacter.org. Set aside some uninterrupted time and complete the character survey.

Once you finish the survey, you will receive a report ranking 24 different character strengths. Take special note of your top 5 strengths.

Ask Other People

Ask a minimum of three to five people what they think your best qualities and strengths are, and also why they feel that way. Include family, friends, co-workers, and bosses; it's great to talk to people from different areas of your life.

Write down the responses you receive. Do they line up with what you think about yourself?

Worksheet 5: Wheel of Life Exercise

Wheel of Life Exercise

The Wheel of Life is a great tool to help you better understand what you can do to add more balance to your life. Think about the eight life categories below. Rate each category from 1 to 10.

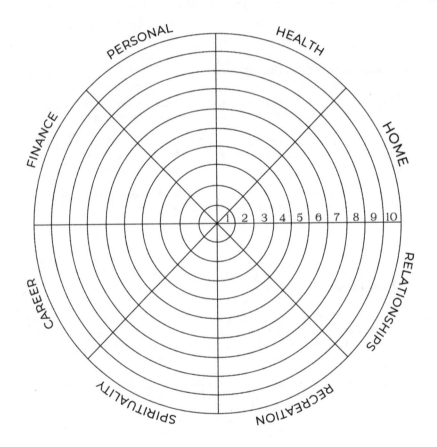

Worksheet 6: Track Your Time, Distractions, and Emotions

Track Your Time, Distractions, and Emotions

Track your activity for five to seven days to collect enough data to understand your natural patterns and habits. Once you're finished, complete the analysis to summarize what you've learned. It's possible to do these exercises simultaneously or separately.

Track Your Time

You can use this worksheet to keep a record of your daily activities. If you forget to fill it out, no need to worry, just try do it as accurately as you can. The purpose of this worksheet is to help you understand how you spend your time and how much time you typically spend on various activities.

Track Your Distractions

Document external distractions like interruptions, email, or the light buzzing in the room. Track internal distractions like daydreaming or losing focus. Identify patterns to plan around and determine which distractions you can control.

Track Your Emotions

Tracking your emotions can provide valuable information about your energy patterns, as well as feelings about certain tasks and activities. Emotions play a significant role in driving ADHD motivation. With a better understanding of how you feel about certain things, you can use this information to plan more effectively.

Analyze the Data

After you have completed enough information to analyze, take some time to answer the corresponding questions to reflect on what you learned. Next, you will take the most important data and fill out the Personal Data Summary worksheet. This will be your cheat sheet while you are building your new planning system.

Worksheet 7: Planning Tools Evaluation

Planning Tools Evaluation

List your current workbox and other tools you use for planning.
Evaluate how the tool is working for you and if you would like to keep
it or find a replacement.

Planning Tools	Reflection Notes	Yes or No

Worksheet 8: Workbox Requirements

Workbox Requirements

Complete the table below of *Must-Haves* and *Nice-to-Haves* for your planning tools. Then you can use this as your cheat sheet when researching new tools for your workbox.

Planning Tools	Must-Haves	Nice-to-Haves

© Take Control ADHD 2024

Worksheet 9: Your Custom Workbox

Your Custom Workbox

This is an outline of your workbox. It includes each tool, the purpose of the tool, and how it connects to the workbox.

Planning Tools	Purpose	Connection

Worksheet 10: Reflections Exercise

Reflections Exercise

Follow this exercise during your Weekly Focus Sessions. Recognize your successes from the week and reflect on how your planning system is working.

Successes

_____

_____

Questions

1. What habits or patterns have you noticed?

_____

_____

2. What do you want to keep doing?

_____

_____

3. What changes do you need to make?

_____

_____

4. Are you on track with your intentional planning for the week? Do you need to make any adjustments?

_____

_____

5. What tasks are you avoiding?

_____

_____

6. What decisions do you need to make this week?

_____

_____

© Take Control ADHD 2024

Worksheet 11: Inbox List

Inbox List

An inbox is where you collect new tasks, projects, and appointments for your calendar. Identify your inboxes and the workflow (action steps) needed to get them into your workbox.

Inbox	Workflow

Worksheet 12: Brain Dump

Brain Dump

Date: _____

Tasks	Priority	Done
_____	(R) (G) (B)	◯
_____	(R) (G) (B)	◯
_____	(R) (G) (B)	◯
_____	(R) (G) (B)	◯
_____	(R) (G) (B)	◯
_____	(R) (G) (B)	◯
_____	(R) (G) (B)	◯
_____	(R) (G) (B)	◯
_____	(R) (G) (B)	◯
_____	(R) (G) (B)	◯
_____	(R) (G) (B)	◯
_____	(R) (G) (B)	◯

Worksheet 13: Planning Workflow Builder

Planning Workflow Builder

Complete the steps below to create a customized workflow.

Chapter 8: Capture and Collect

Action Steps:

1. Scan the area for new incoming information and collect it into one spot.
2. Review inboxes for new incoming information.
3. Enter new information into the workbox.

**List each Inbox to review
during the Weekly Focus**

**List each Inbox to review
during the Daily Detour**

_____   _____

_____   _____

List your action steps for Step 1 for the Weekly Focus

_____

_____

_____

List your action steps for Step 1 for the Daily Detour

_____

_____

_____

Worksheet 14: Intentional Planning Exercise

Intentional Planning Exercise

Start with small steps if you're new to intentional planning or want to try it again. Reflect on how it went at the end of the week.

Directions:

1. Choose one task. Try something easy you know you won't avoid.
2. Schedule a 30-minute time block.
3. Choose a realistic time to do the task.
4. Work with your ADHD. Review your Personal Data Summary for guidance.
5. Set a reminder for 10 minutes before the scheduled time block.
6. Track your progress for later reflection.
7. Write down anything you notice; include notes or ideas to remember.
8. Repeat as often as you would like.

Investigate

Did you do what you said you would do?

_____

_____

How did it feel to get it done? (Identify the benefits)

_____

_____

How did you remember to do the time block?

_____

_____

© Take Control ADHD 2024

Worksheet 15: Weekly Focus Checklist

Weekly Focus Checklist

Complete the steps of the Weekly Focus Checklist. This should take no longer than 30–45 minutes.

Date: _____

☐ _____   ☐ _____

☐ _____   ☐ _____

☐ _____   ☐ _____

☐ _____   ☐ _____

☐ _____   ☐ _____

<u>Notes</u>:

_____

_____

_____

_____

_____

© Take Control ADHD 2024

Worksheet 16: Daily Detour Checklist

Daily Detour Checklist

Take control of your time and spend 10–15 minutes each day to review your
workbox and plan for the day ahead. Make it a great day!

☐ _____   ☐ _____

☐ _____   ☐ _____

☐ _____   ☐ _____

☐ _____   ☐ _____

☐ _____   ☐ _____

<u>Notes:</u>

_____

_____

_____

_____

_____

Worksheet 17: Long-Term Planning

Long-Term Planning

List your rating for each area from your Wheel of Life exercise. Brainstorm the potential projects, tasks, habits, and activities for each area of focus.

AREA	RATING	PROJECTS
PERSONAL		
HEALTH		
HOME		
RELATIONSHIPS		
RECREATION		
SPIRITUALITY		
CAREER		
FINANCE		

© Take Control ADHD 2024

References

ADDA Editorial Team. "ADHD Masking: Does Hiding Your Symptoms Help or Harm?" May 1, 2023, https://add.org/adhd-masking/.

ADDA. "ADHD: The Facts." Attention Deficit Disorder Association, https://add.org/adhd-facts/.

ADDRC. "Using Visual Cues to Remember or Retrieve Information When You Have ADHD." ADD Resource Center, August 27, 2023, https://www.addrc.org/using-visual-cues-to-remember-or-retrieve-information-when-you-have-adhd/.

Aluise, Kelly. "Want a Better Life? Research Says, Start Here." VIA Institute, October 18, 2021, https://www.viacharacter.org/topics/articles/want-a-better-life-research-says-start-here.

"Apple Newton." Wikipedia, accessed January 23, 2024, https://en.wikipedia.org/w/index.php?title=Apple_Newton&oldid=1198278324.

Barkley, Russell. "Executive Function: 7 ADHD Planning, Prioritizing Deficits." ADDitude, October 3, 2019, https://www.additudemag.com/7-executive-function-deficits-linked-to-adhd/.

Blanc, Shawn. "Two types of overwhelm," July 21, 2023, https://shawnblanc.net/category/margin/.

Burkeman, Oliver. Four Thousand Weeks: Time Management for Mortals. Macmillan Audio, 2021.

Cootey, Douglas. "ADHD Hyperfocus Let-Down: Avoiding the Crash." ADDitude, March 31, 2022, https://www.additudemag.com/adhd-hyperfocus-crash/.

Cozzens, Charles F., Norman D. Gardner, and Karen S. Whelan-Berry. "Were the Seven Habits Highly Effective? The Franklin Covey Merger." *Journal of Business Inquiry*, 2005, 15–24.

Dictionary.Com, https://www.dictionary.com.

Dixon, Casey. "Breaking Free of the Burnout Blues with Casey Dixon." *Take Control ADHD*, March 29, 2022, https://takecontroladhd.com/podcast/2410.

Dodson, William. "Rejection Sensitive Dysphoria and ADHD with Dr. Dodson." *Take Control ADHD*, 2019, https://takecontroladhd.com/podcast/405.

Eisenhower Matrix. "Introducing the Eisenhower Matrix," February 7. 2017, https://www.eisenhower.me/eisenhower-matrix/.

"Google Books Ngram Viewer," accessed January 30, 2024, https://books.google.com/ngrams/graph?content=Brain+Dump&year_start=1800&year_end=2019&corpus=en-2019&smoothing=3.

Hall, Karyn. "Radical Acceptance." *Psychology Today*, July 8, 2012, https://www.psychologytoday.com/us/blog/pieces-mind/201207/radical-acceptance.

Hallowell, Edward. "ADHD and Time." Dr. Hallowell, March 2, 2018, https://drhallowell.com/2018/03/02/adhd-and-time-2/.

Hallowell, Edward M., and John J. Ratey. *ADHD 2.0: New Science and Essential Strategies for Thriving with Distraction-from Childhood through Adulthood.* Ballantine Books, 2021.

Honan, Mat. "Remembering the Apple Newton's Prophetic Failure and Lasting Impact." *Wired*, August 5, 2013, accessed 30 January 2024. https://www.wired.com/2013/08/remembering-the-apple-newtons-prophetic-failure-and-lasting-ideals/.

"Impostor Syndrome." Wikipedia, accessed January 27, 2024. https://en.wikipedia.org/w/index.php?title=Impostor_syndrome&oldid=1199702350.

Kosaka H., T. Fujioka, and M. Jung. "Symptoms in individuals with adult-onset ADHD are masked during childhood." *European Archives of Psychiatry and Clinical Neuroscience* 269, no. 6 (2019):753–755. doi: 10.1007/s00406-018-0893-3. Epub April 6, 2018. PMID: 29626225; PMCID: PMC6689273.

Krishna, Priya. "A Guide to Zavarka, Russia's Traditional Tea." *Food & Wine*, accessed January 30, 2024. https://www.foodandwine.com/tea/guide-zavarka-russias-traditional-tea-concentrate.

Lee, Stan, and Steve Ditko. *The Amazing Spider-Man Omnibus*, vol. 1. New York: Marvel, 2007.

Matlen, Terry. *Survival Tips for Women with AD/HD: Beyond Piles, Palms & Post-Its.* Specialty Press, 2005.

McGinnis, Patrick J. https://patrickmcginnis.com/.

"Mind Map." Wikipedia, accessed January 5, 2024. https://en.wikipedia .org/w/index.php?title=Mind_map&oldid=1193784584.

Miserandino, Christine. "But You Don't Look Sick? The Spoon Theory," April 25, 2013. https://butyoudontlooksick.com/articles/written-by-christine/ the-spoon-theory/.

Pedersen, Traci. "Time Blindness: Symptoms, Cause, Tips." *Healthline*, September 29, 2023, https://www.healthline.com/health/time-blindness.

"Planning." Wikipedia, accessed January 27, 2024. https://en.wikipedia .org/w/index.php?title=Planning&oldid=1199498045.

Ochoa, James M. *Focused Forward: Navigating the Storms of Adult ADHD.* Empowering Minds Press, 2016.

Schreckinger, Ben. "The History of FOMO." *Boston* magazine (blog), July 29, 2014. https://www.bostonmagazine.com/news/2014/07/29/fomo-history/.

Shaw, P., A. Stringaris, J. Nigg, and E. Leibenluft. "Emotion dysregulation in attention deficit hyperactivity disorder." *American Journal of Psychiatry* 171, no. 3 (March 2014): 276–93. doi: 10.1176/appi.ajp.2013.13070966. PMID: 24480998; PMCID: PMC4282137.

Solden, Sari, and Michelle Frank. *A Radical Guide for Women with ADHD: Embrace Neurodiversity, Live Boldly, and Break through Barriers.* New Harbinger Publications, 2019.

"Transition." Merriam-Webster, accessed January 28, 2024, https://www .merriam-webster.com/dictionary/transition.

Whitbourne, Kathryn. "What's It Really Like to Have ADHD?" WebMD, July 7, 2021, https://www.webmd.com/add-adhd/features/what-its-like-have-adhd.

Yang, Dmitri. "Perfectionism and ADHD: A Difficult Mix." Care Clinic, n.d., https://careclinic.io/perfectionism-and-adhd/.

Acknowledgments

From Nikki   This book would not have been possible without the wonderful clients I've had the pleasure of working with at Take Control ADHD. It all began with a small beta group where I had an idea about a planning coaching program. The GPS (Guided Planning Sessions) membership was formed with their invaluable assistance. I am immensely grateful to the original members and those who joined later, including those I worked with one on one. You are my inspiration and motivation for the work I do, including this book.

Thank you to my husband, Brad, for always loving me unconditionally. You are my rock and my inspiration to always look at life as a gift and to make each day count. To Jaden and Paige, who call me Mom. I am so incredibly proud of the wonderful human beings you have become. I love you both to the moon and back! Paige, thank you for allowing me to be a part of your journey as you learn about your own unique ADHD mind and your courage to share your story with the TCA ADHD community. And to my dear fur baby, Charlie, who showed up every day alongside me for moral support, I miss you so much.

I am filled with so much love and gratitude toward my dear friends and family for their unwavering support and unconditional love. I cherish these relationships more than anything else in this world and I feel blessed to have you all in my life. I love you.

To Pete, my dear friend. There is no Take Control ADHD without Pete Wright. Thank you for not laughing at me when I called you in 2008 to ask if you were interested in working on my website as a professional organizer. You didn't just do the website; you became a partner. You've always encouraged me to dream bigger. When I asked if I should do a weekly radio show, you said, *How about you do your own podcast with me?* That sounded like fun; 14 years later, we are still doing it. Thank you so much for opening your life with ADHD to our listeners. We make a great team, and I can't imagine doing this with anyone but you. I am so grateful and appreciate you so much!

From Pete Such enormous thanks to my wife, Kira, for her constant loving support of the many, many things I have thrown into the air. Your patience and doggedness in keeping the rest of our lives afloat are what allow projects like this book to see daylight. Could not, would not do any of these things without you in my life. And thanks to my kids—Sophie and Nick—for whom ADHD has become a wondrous competition. I have learned as much from bearing witness to your journey as I have from living through my own. Thank you for your willingness to share and teach along the way.

To Dr. Dodge Rea and Curt Siffert, whose weekly calls were fuel in ways large and small for each chapter of this book. Thank you, old friends.

Thank you to Andy Nelson, business partner and dear friend, for keeping the lights on while I threw hour after hour into this book. You consistently move mountains in our work together, and while I don't understand how you do it, I'm impossibly grateful that you do.

To Nikki, for sharing the opportunity to participate in this book and for your partnership in all that we do together, thank you. I have learned—and continue to learn—about myself and my relationship with my ADHD through our decades of friendship, and I'm deeply grateful to be in your orbit.

From Both Authors   Thank you to Victoria at Wiley for believing we have something to share with the world. We are so grateful for the opportunity; this has been such a wonderful experience. Thank you to the Wiley team for supporting our vision and guiding us when we had many questions. It was a pleasure to experience this with such a supportive team of professionals.

We have immeasurable gratitude for our Take Control ADHD team. It was because of you that we were able to take the time to turn our attention to creating this book. Thank you, Marian Ibrahim and Bryan Brunelle, for your continued dedication and care for the Take Control ADHD Community. And to Melissa Bacheler, our Discord Mom, there simply would have been no operations without you, Operations Manager. We are awed by your inexhaustible energy and will in keeping as many balls in the air as you have juggled. We appreciate you all so much!

Finally, thank you to the Take Control ADHD Patreon community. If you ever stop to ask yourself, "What difference could my little monthly Patreon contributions make to the ADHD team?," know that it makes *all* the difference. It is because of your support of the podcast that this book exists. Thank you for sharing your stories with us and for being a place where others with ADHD can feel heard and safe to be themselves.

From the bottom of our hearts, thank you.

About the Authors

NIKKI KINZER IS a professional certified ADHD coach through the International Coaching Federation (ICF). She's been coaching adults with ADHD since 2010 and has built a business around supporting the ADHD community through coaching, teaching, and podcasting. She lives with her husband, Brad, in Springfield, Oregon.

Pete Wright was diagnosed with ADHD when he was 28 and has spent the better part of his life since then studying and podcasting about his lived ADHD experience. He is a professional podcaster and co-founder of the TruStory FM podcast network. He's a former journalist, educator, and public relations executive and lives with his wife, Kira, in Portland, Oregon.

Index